THE LANCEHEAD SERIES

NEVADA AND THE WEST

Retreat to Nevada

A Socialist Colony of World War I

Retreat to Nevada

A Socialist Colony of World War I

by

WILBUR S. SHEPPERSON

with the assistance of

JOHN G. FOLKES

UNIVERSITY OF NEVADA PRESS · RENO, NEVADA · 1966

UNIVERSITY OF NEVADA PRESS

RENO, NEVADA

© 1966 by University of Nevada Press

Library of Congress Catalog Card Number: 66-63539

DESIGNED BY WILLIAM H. SNYDER

PRINTED IN THE UNITED STATES OF AMERICA

to
Tara Lorraine

Preface

UTOPIAN THOUGHT, populist agitation, and Marxist doctrine have provided students of American life with material for much investigation and debate. Yet one short-lived, but dramatic, episode involving all three of the controversial ideologies has strangely been overlooked. During the trying years of World War I, a series of coincidences combined with the persistent efforts of a few socialists led to the formation of the Nevada Cooperative Colony. The uneasy alliance between utopians, populists, and Marxists quickly dissolved, but not before they had collided with Nevada's patriotic instincts and the encompassing interests of the federal government. Nevertheless, for some two years the small Nevada community provided a magnet which drew hundreds of persons anxious to express dissatisfaction with prevailing institutions.

It was during the spring of 1916 that the socialist promoter C. V. Eggleston secured control of several tracts of farmland in the Lahonton Valley area of Churchill County. Later the same year, Eggleston founded a cooperative society on the J. Scott Harmon ranch some four miles east of Fallon. Almost three dozen houses were constructed over the next two years and the community assumed the name of Nevada City. As a result of nationwide advertising in socialist journals and the support of a diverse assortment of reformers, the colony attracted unusually wide interest and attention. Although always suffering from a rapid turnover in membership, by January, 1918, Nevada City had reached a population of two hundred persons. Clearly, neither the size nor the longevity of the colony would have made it significant. Rather, Nevada City played a peculiar role during World War I by attempting to provide a retreat for antimilitarists, by offering hope to philosophically discouraged reformers, and by reviving a nineteenth-century plan to win the West for the Socialist party.

Despite the public interest and widespread notoriety once accorded the Nevada society, only one printed account describes its activities. In *Communities of the Past and Present*, published in 1924, Ernest Wooster, a member of a closely related colony at Llano, California, devoted some four pages to the Nevada experiment. Lincoln Phifer, a journalist from Girard, Kansas, and a promoter for the Nevada community, prepared a more detailed history, but it was never published. On the other hand, over a dozen studies deal with the mother society at Llano. Publications as diverse as *Desert Magazine*, the *Nation, Sunset*, the *Monthly Review* of the U. S. Bureau of Labor Statistics, the *Los Angeles Times*, and the *California Historical Society Quarterly* have for almost fifty years retold the story of Llano del Rio. Famous authors like Aldous Huxley and Carey McWilliams became intrigued by the tragedy and the drama of the desert utopia. Few of the original records have been found, however, and the sources on the Nevada offspring were so rare that it was either given only a passing note or else ignored altogether.

Although the Nevada colony was an outgrowth of the California experiment, Nevada City and Llano were contemporary and generally competitive societies. Founded in 1914 in the Antelope Valley some forty-five miles northeast of Los Angeles, Llano collapsed and moved to New-llano, Louisiana, in 1917–1918. The Nevada Colony Corporation was organized by former Llano members on April

28, 1916, and although its activity centered at the newly created community of Nevada City, the company lands were never contiguous; they were scattered twelve miles east, twelve miles west, and thirty-five miles north of the society headquarters. The colony went into the hands of receivers on May 1, 1919.

During the forty-five years since the collapse of the Nevada colony, American writers have often discredited utopianism, socialism, and even cooperatives and have thereby contributed to the sense of embarrassment felt by some of the former members of the society. Unfortunately, in the minds of a few people, the sooner all such experiments are forgotten the better. When asked for an interview, a one-time resident of Nevada City replied, "I don't believe in that sort of thing anymore. I'm trying to forget it; I'm still trying to forget it." Nevertheless, by fortunate coincidence the late Senator Patrick A. McCarran gained possession of part of the records of the colony, and through the efforts of his daughter, Sister Margaret Patricia, they have been deposited in the Nevada Historical Society. The McCarran Papers, along with the recent discovery by the University of Nevada library of the community's newspaper, the *Co-op-erative Colonist*, and the friendly assistance of many persons who were associated with or remember the experiment, provide the basis for the present study.

Grateful acknowledgment is made to twenty Nevadans who supplied noteworthy accounts of Nevada City, the Lahonton Valley, or the socialist temperament during World War I. Persons interviewed at Fallon were Gordon Barkley, A. T. Baumann, Ernest L. Baumann, Martha Baumann, Leland Ellis, Phillip Hiibel, Sam Hiibel, Fred Kirn, and William Pierce. Those interviewed in Reno and Sparks were James Bailey, Margaret Schneider Eikelberger, Mel Hancock, Melvin Jepson, Ernie Kormier, S. R. Marean, Charles Miller, Samuel Platt, Artie Riggle, Henry Schneider, and Lottie Kormier Vulgamore. S. M. Watts of Pittsburg, Kansas, made a special contribution through his personal assessment of Fred D. Warren, Lincoln Phifer, and Ben Wilson.

The writer is particularly indebted to Sister Margaret Patricia for providing much of the primary material for the study, and to the staff of the Nevada Historical Society for arranging the McCarran Papers and making other records and documents easily accessible. Professors Russell R. Elliott, James W. Hulse, and Paul H. Smith of the University of Nevada have given freely of their time and have been most helpful on matters of both content and style.

W. S. S.

Reno, Nevada
January, 1966

Contents

xiii

Contents

Retreat to Nevada

A Socialist Colony of World War I

Overview

THE TRAVELER does not come easily to the decayed village of Nevada City, Nevada. The empty field is served by neither a wagon trail nor a footpath. It is a landscape which no longer suggests that human beings once viewed the scene as a universal panorama from which man could rekindle his hopes. Now, brambles and burrs, brush and sand, a barbed-wire fence, and a wide irrigation ditch bar the approach to the village. The adobe houses have dissolved into clay plateaus two or three feet high, giving the scene the appearance of an ancient fortification. Yet it has been only forty-five years since the site was filled with human activity—since the broken pieces of crockery and glass, the battered washtubs and rusty bed springs, the old shoes and corset stays performed a useful function in the pattern of life. For over four decades the dust has blown along Euclid Avenue, and the rain has melted down the friable walls. In the spring, tumbleweeds and nettles grow among the houses and over them. Greasebrush, four or five feet high, now obscures the plan of the town.

Overview

Fortunately, the disasters of history quickly merge into
the dramatic, the colorful, and the romantic, and most of the
personal tragedy surrounding Nevada's World War I venture into socialism has been forgotten. Today, nearly all of
the more than five hundred and fifty residents who settled
in the community have vanished, and the nearly two thousand people who became members in absentia have destroyed
their worthless stock certificates. The group of antiwar Germans who saw the colony as an escape from "capitalistic
militarism" were among the first to become disillusioned;
the scores of Oklahomans who threatened to turn Lahonton
Valley into a setting for *The Grapes of Wrath* have long
since scattered. Indeed, it seems incredible that a sandy
waste four miles east of Fallon could have, within a few
action-packed months, attracted persons from thirty-three
states, Alaska, Hawaii, Cuba, Canada, England, Germany,
Sweden, France, Hungary, and Switzerland.

In the half-century before World War I, a hundred thousand miners had left Nevada with a hundred ghost towns as
a reminder of their search for quick gain. But Nevada City
represented a search for economic interdependence and human dignity. Perhaps its plans for an arcadian valley were
more nearly symbolic of the hopes of the average pioneer
than the well publicized boom camps of frontier days. It,
like the famed mining camps, progressed rapidly from a
tent village to wooden buildings and eventually to adobe-
brick structures. But in every other respect it differed from
the mining towns: guns did not blaze in the streets; prospec-
tors did not coax their burros toward the hills; an abundance
of water flowed through miles of surrounding irrigation
ditches; there was not a single saloon or gambling hall or
prostitute. Of the more than three hundred deserted Ne-

vada communities, none enjoyed greater hopes, a more permanent source of wealth, or more humane expectations.

Nevada City also played a role in the larger program of socialism. The community was not only the legal outgrowth of the famed Llano colony of California but also an intellectual outgrowth of Laurence Gronlund's *The Co-operative Commonwealth* (1884) and of the Brotherhood of the Co-operative Commonwealth organized in 1895. The colony ties with early utopian doctrines paved the way for its acceptance among leading publicists and reformers throughout the United States. In the final instance the colony reflected an unusual phase in Nevada history. It climaxed an era of ill-advised settlement schemes, of federal reclamation projects, and of violent labor disturbances. With the collapse of the colony, not only socialism but rural radicalism succumbed in Nevada.

No doubt the society projected a philosophy of life and provided a framework for action which appealed to the colonists. However, most who were drawn to the colony went because they did not have concrete answers to practical questions. They sought survival in a helter-skelter world. For many Americans, primitive conditions still existed; they found themselves pitted against nature on dry and windswept farms in Oklahoma or Dakota or Idaho. Such people had suffered from overwork and had endured the loneliness of the frontier. They were in need of a purposeful approach to life. It was more a personal problem than a conflict with society, more their dull and dreary existence than a glowing picture of the future, which led them to Nevada City. Other colonists were pitted against American social organization. They had come to reject many of the dominant institutional forms like church affiliation, politi-

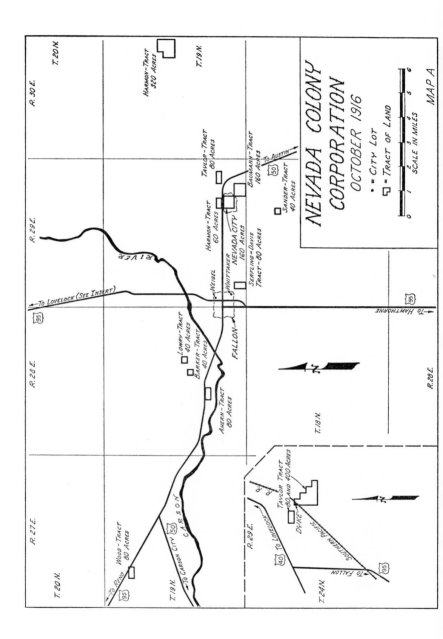

NEVADA COLONY
CORPORATION
OCTOBER 1916

• = CITY LOT
□ = TRACT OF LAND

SCALE IN MILES
0 1 2 3 4 5 6

MAP A

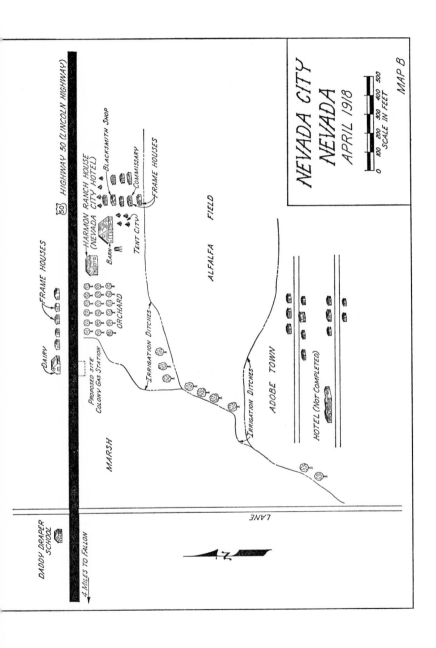

NEVADA CITY
NEVADA
APRIL 1918

SCALE IN FEET
0   100 200 300 400 500

MAP B

cal participation, or economic capitalism. They were eagerly searching for a means to provide the basic needs for survival. Many were attracted by the colony propaganda. It was pitched low; its distinctiveness came from plainness. People came to believe that ordinary experiences when conducted cooperatively could bring a contentment, a satisfaction, and a success not to be found in the competitive world.

The educated and literary colonists always insisted that they were not utopians, but realists and naturalists in the tradition of Frank Norris, Theodore Dreiser, Charles Edward Russell, or Julius Wayland. They were, however, hopelessly inconsistent. They scoffed at the old mythology, yet retained Horatio Alger as a hero. They regarded capitalism as an idol to be smashed, yet demonstrated economic orthodoxy in the formation of the colony. They ridiculed puritanism, yet remained steadfastly puritan. And while arguing the sylvan virtues of rural America, they accepted the inevitability of progress with its road to industrialization.

In the decades before 1914, utopian movements absorbed much from the contemporary socialist doctrines, but they also were influenced by such formulas for the good life as universal suffrage, prohibition, and Montessori schools. The Nevada colony brought together these mercurial and often contradictory trends and attempted to unify them into a practicable program. The community was not utopian in the traditional sense and differed from most similar experiments in that it was never overstocked with visionary leaders. The theorists, agitators, and armchair pundits were a small minority when contrasted with the tradesmen, artisans, laborers, and the large body of experienced farmers. The colony promoters promised community comradeship, better training for the youth, political control of Nevada,

and, most significant, greater material prosperity. They believed that the profit motive had failed; yet at the core of
the cooperative there was always a perfectly frank desire
for an improved economic position. Colony writers explained that competition, not wealth, was the chief cause
of the widespread distress; therefore, with competition abol-
ished and profitable employment available for all, harmony
would prevail.

Assured and reassured that the future belonged to those
who dared to venture, the isolated and the idealists, the
transient and the anonymous were drawn to Nevada City.
For three years, colony life pulsed and throbbed with rich
drama and rough dialogue. Nothing was static. But instead
of maturing into a prosperous communal conservatism, the
society was always plagued by uncertainty, individualism,
and anarchy.

Crumbling walls, discarded utensils, and streets choked
with weeds and brush symbolize the defeat of those who
once envisioned Nevada City. But the colony was more than
an unfortunate blunder, more than an insignificant encounter. Although it was a mistake, the effort was not in
vain unless life's dream of happiness and paradise is a wasted
fancy.

Chapter I

California Backdrop
and the
Nevada Colony Corporation

As COFOUNDERS of the Nevada experiment, Job Harriman and C. V. Eggleston were caught up in the hodgepodge of utopian thinking and communitarianism which had for centuries excited the mind of Western man. From Plato to Saint Augustine to Sir Thomas More, dreams of the perfect society had animated the lives of reformers. Such dreams gave men not truth but purpose, not a historical validity but an intelligible sparkle, not sustained success but subtle meaning. With the discovery of America, the pursuit of paradise assumed a more tangible and exaggerated form. America became the land of quests.

AMERICAN COOPERATIVE COLONIES

For more than three hundred years, idealists sought to harmonize man with his environment through the creation of backwoods utopias. By 1916, at least two hundred and fifty cooperative communities had been established in the United

States, but more than half had collapsed in infancy. Despite the short life of a majority of the American societies, each new generation brought a new wave of experiments. Communal groups resembled the life cycle in that the real proof of their vitality seemed to be not in continuance, but in rebirth. Many experiments like Fruitlands, Brook Farm, and New Harmony survived but a few months; yet in their endeavor to take life apart and reassemble it with greater perfection, their influence was incalculable.

The more durable American colonies of Ephrata, the Shakers, the Rappists, and Amana, all of which functioned for more than a hundred years, were belated outgrowths of the Reformation. They attempted to dig to the roots of Christianity and practice the fundamentals of their faith. An imitation of Jesus accounted for the longevity of such communities. But the Reformation provided a second and more subtle stimulus to cooperation. It opened the door to a reassessment of political and material values and to an eventual outcry against the tyranny, poverty, and ugliness of life. When the industrial revolution further contributed to the physical and spiritual enslavement of man, the groundwork was laid for the great age of cooperative experiments.

By the early nineteenth century, social reformers like Robert Owen, Étienne Cabet, and François Fourier were attracting wide attention, but their communal organizations were tragically ill-advised. They prepared the way, however, for the next generation of American cooperators. In the twenty years from 1870 to 1890, some forty-five utopian novels emphasized economic maladjustments and the unequal distribution of wealth.[1] In most of the books a solution was offered whereby all the ills of society were to be swept away through the application of some infallible formula—usually the cooperative idea. Limited association through farm-mutual societies, benefit organizations, home and foreign missions, temperance leagues, and producer cooperatives became widespread.

The farmers' Grange was founded in 1866; after the depression of 1873 it organized numerous cooperatives for marketing, for collective buying, and for the production of agricultural machinery. Although eclipsed as a political force by the Farmers' Alliances, the Grange survived as a social agency and during the 1890's played a significant role in the formation of farmer cooperatives throughout the northern plains states. While the Grange fostered rural cooperation, various workingmen's groups combined European and American doctrines in an attempt to promote united action among urban workers. The most famous cooperative program of the 1880's was that of the Nationalist Clubs (inspired by ideas set forth in Edward Bellamy's utopian novel, *Looking Backward*). As the Nationalist Clubs dissolved about 1890, Daniel DeLeon and some of Bellamy's followers turned to militant socialism while other Nationalists joined the populist movement and gave the People's party a distinct utopian appeal. In the election of 1892 the populists were victorious in four western states, and in Nevada they carried every county except Douglas.

Throughout the same period, new and volatile foreign doctrines and ideologies merged with native thought to emphasize the capitalist disregard for the community. Labor disturbances, depressions, and rural discontent provided the new movements with ready followers. Exploitation of natural resources, political dishonesty and favoritism, the control of wealth by big business, the collapse of populism, an upsurge in protest literature, and a new sense of humanitarianism further emphasized the need for a new assessment of society.

By the end of the nineteenth century, the American West and particularly California had become the mecca for scores of bizarre social experiments. The towns of Riverside, Banning, Long Beach, Westminster, Anaheim, Farmersville, and San Diego were founded as cooperative enterprises. There was the Italian-Swiss colony at Asti, a Japanese colony in Sonoma County, the Russian Quakers in the Los Angeles area, English colonies, Polish settlements, Scandinavian cooperatives, theosophical communities, the Bergenroth dictatorship, communist organizations, agricultural cooperatives, the Sawmill-Relief projects, Unemployed Exchange associations, Self-Help societies, and Rochdale Cooperative stores. California had become the home of the new, the bold, and the utopian.[2]

JOB HARRIMAN

In 1886, at the height of the colony movement, Job Harriman arrived in California. He quickly became an advocate of both the cooperative and socialist programs, and after a brief association with the Altrurian colony in the mid-1890's, he emerged as the leading political figure of California socialism.

In 1894, a community, which took its name from the William Dean Howells essay "A Traveler from Altruria," was formed on Mark West Creek near Santa Rosa. Edward Biron Payne, a Christian Socialist who tied the doctrines of Karl Marx to those of Jesus Christ, laid down the philosophy for Altruria. Payne, once a Congregational minister in Berkeley, had become a Unitarian, but finally had accepted

12

the Altrurian creed of saving society before saving the individual. The belief was further complicated by a Calvinistic determination to turn the world into the Kingdom of God, but was tempered by an enlightened and optimistic view of man and his eagerness to reform when given the proper motivation. Altruria formed several branch agencies throughout the area, and cooperative stores were organized.

In the spring of 1895, the manager of the San Francisco store moved to the parent colony in Sonoma Valley, and Job Harriman was selected as president of the San Francisco Altrurian council.[3] The experience with a bakery, laundry, commissary, and other cooperative services made an indelible impression upon Harriman and influenced him in the formation of Llano two decades later. He never quite divorced himself from the strange Altrurian brand of Christian Marxism. Harriman believed that socialism could succeed through gradual change and education, and that economic control and social reorientation could assure a political victory by the Socialist party. He later explained: "I assumed that if a co-operative colony could be established in which an environment were created that would afford each individual an equal and social advantage, that they would, in a comparatively short time, react harmoniously to this environment and the conflicting interests would be done away."[4]

Born on an Indiana farm in 1861, Harriman, like his mentor Payne, first studied to be a preacher, but left Northwest Christian University (now Butler University) for Colorado College. Later he returned to Indiana and was admitted to the bar in 1885. He moved to California the following year, and soon became one of the commanding advocates of western socialism. After his experiences with

Altrurian cooperatives in the mid-1890's, he ran for governor of California in 1898 but received only 5,143 votes.[5] In 1899, a large faction broke from the Socialist Labor party and set up headquarters at Rochester, New York. Harriman was selected by the Socialist Labor "Kangaroos" in early 1900 as their presidential nominee; however, in March the dissidents attended the Social Democratic convention. In a partial merger of the two groups, Harriman accepted the nomination for the vice-presidency, sharing the ticket with Eugene V. Debs. When the combined organization received 96,000 votes, Socialists became convinced that victory could be achieved through direct political action rather than in the "thorny desert of utopianism."

Harriman had moved to Los Angeles before the election, and after defeat threw himself into the local labor movement. He participated in the bitter and extended Los Angeles dispute between labor and management and opposed the coalition "reform government" which was formed in 1910. The coalition quickly showed itself to be as anti-union as the earlier employer-dominated city council. At the height of the confusion, on October 1, 1910, the *Los Angeles Times* building was dynamited. Twenty-one persons were killed and scores injured. The city council immediately engineered the arrest of hundreds of pickets and labor leaders. The labor organizers, James B. and John J. McNamara, were unofficially seized in Indianapolis and returned to California to stand trial, along with Artie McManigal, for the bombing. Harriman not only joined with Clarence Darrow to defend the McNamara brothers, he also became a candidate for mayor on a joint Labor and Socialist ticket. The pro-Labor chances for victory appeared excellent until on December 1, 1911, the McNamara brothers pleaded guilty to the bombing. Five days later the Socialist-Labor coalition was defeated; Harriman received 51,000 out of approximately 140,000 votes cast.

After three major political defeats, Harriman became convinced that economic success must precede political control if socialism were to become a reality. Furthermore, economic recession was spreading throughout the West. As unemployment increased, tension mounted. Both the Industrial Workers of the World and vigilante leaders were growing more daring and determined. Incidents like the one at Durst farm near Wheatland, California, when a district attorney, a deputy sheriff, and two workers were killed, and the National Guard was called out, only dramatized the chaos. The "Corey Army" of fifteen hundred unemployed workers left San Francisco on the first leg of a proposed march on Washington, but were informed in Sacramento that the governor of Nevada would turn them back at Reno by force. San Diego, Fresno, and Stockton had major disturbances. In the midst of the 1913 turmoil, Job Harriman again ran for mayor of Los Angeles and again lost to a Progressive-Republican coalition.[6]

THE LLANO COLONY

Even before the campaign of 1913, Harriman and a few close associates had determined that the time was propitious for putting socialism into action. Experience with farm cooperatives coupled with urban political failures pointed the way to the creation of a rural colony. Tracts of land were considered in Oregon, Arizona, Nevada, and California. Harriman almost purchased a large estate in San Luis Obispo County, and the Reno and Fallon regions of Nevada were studied carefully. But he eventually decided on an arid arm of the Mojave Desert extending north of the San Gabriel Mountains, known as Antelope Valley. Writers have been fond of picturing the tall, ascetic intellectual overlooking his proposed community with field glasses and speculating on the beauty which would draw those of an artistic temperament, the fertility which would draw the practical farmer, and the climate which would invigorate everyone.[7] Although located in northern Los Angeles County only forty-five air miles from the city, the mesa was over ninety miles by road, and twenty miles from the railroad at Palmdale. The tract consisted of some nineteen thousand acres of sagebrush, yuccas, creosote bush, and scrub junipers.

In 1880, a temperance group had launched a community at the same site but had abandoned the area because of a shortage of water. Late in the 1880's, the Big Rock Irrigation District organized and sold $240,000 worth of bonds for the construction of a tunnel that was to bring water from the Big Rock Creek. The project was short-lived.[8] By 1914, the Mescal Land and Water Company had become a major property owner in the valley. After extensive publicity, Harriman and eight business partners, two of whom were bankers, arranged to purchase both the property and the Mescal company for $80,000 but made only a very small down payment.

In the meantime, the Llano del Rio Company was organized with a capitalization of two million dollars. Capital stock was to be sold only to those who intended to live in the colony. There were two companies, therefore, with an interlocking directorship. The Mescal company, which originally held the land, slowly transferred its stock to the Llano company. Of 50,000 shares of Mescal stock, Llano held 44,222 by December 31, 1915; but by the same date, 44,222 shares of the Llano stock had been transferred to Mescal as payment for the land. More significant, the Mescal company purchased land and transferred it to Llano at a profit while at the same time using the stock paid by Llano as the collateral for the purchase in the first place.[9] Llano, therefore, was a socialistic colony created through the use of many devious capitalistic devices and designed in part to provide a profit for the associates who had secured the Mescal company.

The colony was officially launched with five members, four horses, one cow, and six hogs on May Day, 1914.[10] The initial response to socialism in action was most encouraging. Trouble spots in the central valley produced a particularly large number of applicants, and extensive advertising and speaking tours created interest throughout the West. Some 60 to 70 percent of the members of the community were drawn from west of the Rocky Mountains, with over 25 percent coming from California. Some 40 percent were farmers.[11] The organization was not designed for the poor or needy, and as the months passed, Harriman found that the well-to-do manifested less selfishness than the lower classes. The board of directors passed on each applicant, and if approved—all with the necessary cash were accepted —the prospective member contracted to purchase two thousand shares of stock at one dollar per share. Five hundred dollars was paid in cash and the remainder by deducting one dollar per day from a four-dollar–per–day wage. Living expenses for the member and his family were subtracted from the remaining three dollars with any balance accruing as credits to be paid, eventually, from the profits of the colony. Not more than seventy-five dollars in profits were to be paid in any one year to any one stockholder, however. There was a guarantee of continuous employment with annual vacations of two weeks. Members might use outside funds to purchase any luxuries or necessities they wished as long as such purchases did not interfere with the community system of production and distribution.

Difficulties in housing, transportation, supply, and organization of the labor battalion quickly became apparent. Nevertheless, a dormitory, hotel, bakery, laundry, printing plant, bath house, poultry house, silo, and other buildings were completed. Colony leaders devised extensive plans for growing alfalfa, potatoes, and melons, and at one point it was suggested that the producing and canning of pears would in itself meet the financial needs of the society. One hundred and twenty acres were devoted to pear orchards, eighty acres to apples, and large areas to other fruit. Swimming, dancing, music, and other recreation and sports were emphasized, and as the population grew, state and local officials cooperated in opening a grammar school.

The management viewed the printing and publicity operation as one of the most significant departments. A year before the colony was launched, Harriman secured control of the *Western Comrade*, a Los Angeles monthly edited by Emanuel Julius. Frank E. Wolfe quickly replaced Julius as editor and converted the periodical into a thirty-two-page publicity brochure for Llano. Articles by Carl Sandburg, Edwin Markham, and leading socialists, along with items on sex, temperance, and labor conditions, interspersed the advertisements. Emphasis was placed on labor unrest in the central valley, and California authorities were compared to Texas lynch mobs. But despite the reference, it was made clear that at Llano only Caucasians were to be admitted. Applications from "Negroes, Hindus, Mongolians and Malays" had been disapproved because such people had no place in "the greatest community enterprise ever launched in America."[12] Later, when the colony moved to Louisiana and it became necessary to employ Negroes to work at the local sawmill, a separate drinking cup was kept for "blacks" and their treatment in general was harsh and often abusive.[13]

Although the colony was not self-sufficient, and in fact survived on the five-hundred-dollar cash payments advanced by new members, both single persons and families continued to crowd the community's rudimentary facilities. By 1916, the colony claimed more than nine hundred residents. Local publicity, however, exaggerated most facets of cooperative life, and the constant movement in and out gave the colony the appearance of a boom town and made it easy to overestimate the permanent population. Of course not all residents of Llano were unselfish supporters of the administration. Internal dissension followed within a few months of the initial settlement. The critics banded together in a welfare league and attacked the autocratic control of Harriman and his board of directors. The league was in part responsible for a 1915 investigation of the colony by the California commissioner of corporations.

While the Llano del Rio Company was being formed, California enacted the Corporate Securities Act commonly known as the "blue sky" law. The purpose was to provide investors in securities greater protection by allowing the sale of capital stock only after a corporation secured a permit from, and underwent an investigation by, the state. Complaints charging the Llano directors with inept management had been received by the commissioner of corporations late in 1914. Consequently, Commissioner H. L. Carnahan appointed his deputy commissioner in Los Angeles, H. W. Bowman, to investigate, analyze, and prepare a report on colony affairs. After seven months, Bowman and an assistant issued their findings on December 31, 1915. The report was highly critical of colony financing, accounting, and management. The company's books showed debts on land totaling more than ninety thousand dollars, but more significant, the expenditures for food, livestock feed, and other necessities were taken from the cash payments of persons entering the organization and not from colony production. Therefore, as the colony grew, more and more persons would have to buy stock to pay for the increasing amount of food consumed. It was an ever-mounting spiral which could lead only to bankruptcy. The state commissioner agreed to grant the corporation a permit to sell stock only after a copy of the Bowman report was shown to prospective purchasers and significant changes in the organization had been instituted. Harriman would not meet the commissioner's demands and turned to C. V. Eggleston for assistance in chartering the company under Nevada law.[14]

C. V. EGGLESTON

No doubt much of the fame and growth experienced by Llano can be credited to the company's fiscal agent, C. V. Eggleston. As the organizer-director of the Nevada colony, Eggleston proved to be one of the most dynamic, elusive, and controversial cooperators of the period. Even persons who worked closely with "old C. V." failed to understand his methods or learn much of his past. Slender in stature, of medium height, bald, and sickly, he was nearing sixty years of age when he arrived in Nevada. Although apparently a native of Oklahoma, he had lived in California for many years. As president of the Eggleston-King Pigeon Company of Oakland, he and his partners, W. I. DeLong and C. A. King, bred and sold squabs and fancy pigeons in San Francisco and Los Angeles. In early 1914, the business was disbanded, and Eggleston moved to Los Angeles. He became a notary public in November and soon thereafter accepted the post as advertising manager and fiscal agent for the Llano colony.

By April, 1915, Eggleston's name even began to replace Harriman's as the author of lead articles in the *Western Comrade*. His salesmanship was explosive, catchy, and effective. With headlines reading "Wanted: 600 Men," he was sure to gain the attention of thousands of California's unemployed.[15] But Eggleston's propaganda was directed at avowed socialists with some wealth; he did not waste time trying to convert capitalists. Indeed, his greatest effort was directed toward attracting educated socialist leaders—they were used as agents in selling the program.

Eggleston was a talker, a persuader, and a salesman with such hypnotic qualities that farmers deeded him their land, urban employees wrote him personal checks, and socialist editors declared him a modern day pathfinder. His self-assurance bordered on arrogance; his grey eyes were as "emphatic as steel." While always respected even by his bitterest enemies, he seems to have endeared himself to no one. Swift and agile physically as well as mentally, he boasted that if mice were placed under an inverted box on a table and then the box quickly lifted he could catch all of the animals before they reached the edge of the table.[16] He lectured youthful friends on life adjustment and the path to success. Even though he deliberately kept poor records, no detail escaped him whether it was the repairing of an automobile, the making of a bed, or the delivering of a speech. He was a master of the quick-sell, yet he emphasized "sell" even if you have to make "a dozen trips." He counseled his close Nevada associate, L. V. Flowers, "think success and the business will come, the more confidence you have in yourself the easier it will be for you to transfer that confidence to the people you meet."[17] Although a socialist, Eggleston was a hearty exponent of American pragmatism.

Eggleston's name was dropped from the *Western Comrade* after August, 1915, and it was hinted at Llano that he had been relieved of his position because of questionable methods. Actually, the master salesman arrived in Nevada in September, 1915, and quickly organized the Nevada Colony Corporation so that the Llano company could incorporate under Nevada law. It is uncertain whether Eggleston was sent to Nevada for the express purpose of forming the new corporation, or whether he sensed the criticism that was to come from the commissioner of corporations in California and deliberately located in Nevada so that his service would become indispensable to Harriman.

THE NEVADA COLONY CORPORATION

Eggleston visited western Nevada in early 1915 and was immediately impressed by the physical and human potential of the area. Upon being relieved as agent at Llano in August, 1915, he immediately returned to Reno and laid the groundwork for the Nevada cooperative. Three fellow salesmen from Llano drew up the Articles of Incorporation in Los Angeles on September 21. Thomas Smalley was designated president, and L. V. Flowers secretary; they then forwarded the documents to Reno where Eggleston persuaded A. Grant Miller, head of the Socialist party in Nevada, to accept the post of attorney and resident agent for the new society. Drafted on October 6, the petition legalizing the Nevada Colony Corporation was filed with the secretary of state on October 12, 1915.

The articles of incorporation authorized the issuing of five million dollars in capital stock at one dollar per share. When two thousand shares were sold, the company was to begin operations. Since the three Los Angeles salesmen had purchased two thousand shares on October 6, registration by the secretary of state activated the corporation.[18] (See Appendix C for articles of incorporation.)

Although Eggleston was in fact the creator of the Nevada Colony Corporation, at this point he was not officially associated with it. Instead, he had become president of a related organization entitled the Union Security Company. The latter company's articles of incorporation drawn up at Los Angeles on November 15, 1915, were identical to those of the Nevada Colony Corporation except that they emphasized the fiscal and escrow nature of the new association. Capitalized at $200,000, the Union Security Company's petition for incorporation was filed with the secretary of state on December 6, 1915. The officers were: C. V. Eggleston, president; L. V. Flowers, secretary; A. Grant Miller, resident agent; and Gentry P. McCorkle, the third stockholder. (McCorkle withdrew from the company in September, 1916, and through legal maneuvering later gained personal control of the Llano property.) Thus, by the end of 1915, Eggleston had devised a corporate structure almost identical to the one he had known at Llano. The Union Security Company, like the Mescal Land and Water Company, was an outside agency designed to purchase land, sell stock, and conduct helpful negotiations for the major colony corporation.

Although passing references had been made to a colony to be located near Fallon in Churchill County, it was not until February, 1916, that local newspapers began to publicize the society. Eggleston returned to Reno from a trip to Los Angeles on February 8 and announced that he was anxious to purchase land upon which to locate one thousand families. He revealed a close association with Job Harriman and explained that the new Nevada colony would be an equal partner with the Llano del Rio Company in the ownership of all property in Nevada and California. Indeed, upon becoming a member the Nevada colonist would immediately and automatically gain a share in the Los Angeles County holdings. The *Western Comrade* of Llano was to move to Nevada as quickly as a suitable location could be arranged, and a series of socialist lectures throughout the United States was to publicize the Nevada settlement.[19]

Over the following weeks Socialist activity blended with colony promotion to further dramatize the impending immigration to Nevada. A daily socialist newspaper was scheduled to start publication at Reno in April, and Emil Seidel, the Socialist vice-presidential candidate of 1912, traveled to Nevada on a lecture tour. On February 29, only four days after Seidel's talk, A. Grant Miller and C. V. Eggleston conducted a meeting at Eagle's Hall, Reno, to announce that agreements had been made for establishing the new colony at Fallon. Miller had for some time been credited with being a "great booster" for the state, and the colony idea was presented as "a marvelous demonstration of the possibilities of practical co-operation."[20]

Eggleston's claim that the Nevada colonists would own a share in the Los Angeles colony was soon verified. On March 13, 1916, the 369,037 shares of capital stock issued by the Llano del Rio Company of California were conveyed to the Nevada Colony Corporation. The astute Harriman, however, demanded $82,000 in payment for his company's property, but since the Nevada Colony Corporation had no funds, it merely issued Nevada Colony Corporation stock to the California group. Rather surprisingly, the individual depositions authorizing the transfer of stock to Nevada showed Eggleston to be the largest shareholder in the old Llano company. Indeed, Eggleston owned 30,306 shares in Llano whereas the next largest stockholder held only 3,581 shares. Job Harriman claimed only 1,610 shares at the time of transfer, and other founder-directors had an even smaller investment in the Llano corporation.[21] Obviously the system of selling stock on commission had made Eggleston the most powerful force in the company and had contributed to Harriman's decision to rid himself of the salesman in August, 1915.

Eggleston's extensive holdings at Llano, coupled with his dominant position in Nevada, led to a temporary compromise between him and the Southern California interests. Harriman became president of the Nevada Colony Corporation, and four of his old associates took over official posts in the company. Eggleston became vice-president and general manager, and his associate, L. V. Flowers, became secretary. A. Grant Miller remained attorney and legal counsel. In addition, Eggleston was to be responsible for locating and building the new Nevada colony.

In the meantime, the Llano-Fallon partnership gave added prestige to the Nevada colony idea, and the belief by socialists that they were investing in land in Los Angeles County as well as in Churchill County led many to buy stock in the venture. Eggleston's motives appear clear. He hoped to build a colony in Nevada to rival that of California; since all legal activities were centered in Nevada and since he personally held more than thirty thousand shares of stock in Llano, it seemed that in a few months he could control the entire movement. In addition, it quickly became obvious that Eggleston planned to use his personal organization, the Union Security Company, as the fiscal agent for the entire operation.

Many of the California-based directors arrived in Reno in early April, 1916, and on April 14 Job Harriman, A. F. Snell, W. A. Engle, and Frank Wolfe were conducted around Fallon and shown the colony property secured by Eggleston. The trip apparently convinced Harriman that Eggleston might well be able to gain control of the entire organization unless an immediate and dramatic step was taken. Therefore, at the first annual stockholders meeting of the Nevada Colony Corporation, held in Miller's law office in Reno on April 18 and 19, Harriman dictated the choice of the new directors. All were his Llano men. The new board immediately selected a new slate of officers which excluded all of the Nevada group from the governing body. Gentry P. McCorkle, having assured Harriman of his loyalty, was reelected a director and remained as treasurer; Miller was retained as resident agent. A further action of the April 18 and 19 stockholders' meeting authorized the new directors to change the name of the organization from the Nevada Colony Corporation to the Llano del Rio Company of Nevada. With official registration the new title became effective on April 28, 1916, and the brief era of close association between the California and Nevada interests was ended.

At the April 18 and 19 meeting, Eggleston shrewdly refrained from waging a losing struggle with Harriman and instead arranged a compromise. Before the name change was effected, the Nevada Colony Corporation transferred to Eggleston's Union Security Company all of the Nevada and Northern California property that had been acquired over the previous few months. In return, Eggleston cooperated in the formation of the Llano del Rio Company of Nevada. Eggleston's son, E. G. Eggleston, who had become a Washoe County notary public, even authenticated many of the documents affecting the company's name change.[22] Eggleston, of course, had no intention of allowing his Nevada enterprises to collapse with the exodus of the California group; rather, he engaged in legal trickery. On April 28, 1916, within a few hours after the Nevada Colony Corporation officially became the Llano del Rio Company of Nevada, he founded a new Nevada Colony Corporation with articles of incorporation identical with those of the old company. Three days later, on May 1, 1916, the new Nevada Colony Corporation held its organizational meeting.

Eggleston had jealously guarded his Nevada undertaking from the first and had often delayed turning over property to the old corporation. In at least one instance, rather than issuing Nevada Colony Corporation stock in exchange for property, he returned the deeds to the owner.[23] More often, however, the Union Security Company functioned as a transfer agent where titles were temporarily held. Some of the arrangements with property owners had been made deliberately vague. For example, on April 24, 1916, N. C. and Ethel E. Whitaker consented to trade two horses, one cow, two sets of harness, one wagon, farm and blacksmith tools, thirty-three hens, one stand of bees, eleven rabbits, and one lot in Fallon with a house on it to Eggleston for one thousand shares of capital stock in the Union Security Company. But the agreement stipulated that "as soon as a new company shall be incorporated with plans and purposes the same as the Nevada Colony Corporation we agree to exchange share for share the said Union Company stock for stock in said new company." The entire transaction was recorded with pencil on a piece of scratch paper and in Eggleston's almost illegible handwriting.[24]

For the first four months of 1916, Eggleston had been able to trade upon the Harriman prestige and the Llano name. Few persons understood the developments of late April, and, with the Nevada group retaining the company name, it was often assumed that Eggleston had become head of the entire cooperative enterprise. Furthermore, Eggleston had gained possession of considerable property, the cooperation of local socialist organizations, the active participation of the popular A. Grant Miller, and the support of many socialist leaders of national prominence. The formation, promotion, and orientation of the Fallon community had been deftly handled, but it remained to be seen whether Eggleston's management of the society would be equally astute.

THE COLLAPSE OF LLANO

After April 28, 1916, Llano was no longer legally associated with the Nevada experiment. However, both were incorporated under Nevada law, and the two were closely related in the public mind. Furthermore, the movement of colonists and the exchange of colony stock tended to bring the societies into a spirited competition. The disintegration of the California project and its transfer to Louisiana was of particular significance in the development of Nevada City.

Although involved in law suits and suffering from internal discontent, Llano managed to survive until confronted by the water shortage of 1917.[25] Engineers and surveyors had initially assured Harriman that the mountains could supply adequate water for the irrigation of thousands of acres as well as the needs of a small city. But they failed to reckon with the San Andreas fault, the porous soil, the extensive evaporation, and the water rights already held by neighboring ranchers. Dams and reservoirs were the subject of constant discussion, and a few minor works were completed. Several irrigation ditches were lined with stone and paved with concrete, and channels east of Big Rock Creek were cleared despite the violent objections of farmers to the west who claimed the water. Water was even transported by truck and teams, but eventually it became painfully obvious that the "largest socialist colony in the United States" was confronted with an insurmountable obstacle.

In early 1917, Harriman started his search for a more propitious location. Again attention was given to Oregon, Arizona, and a fertile tract near Modesto, California. There was considerable discussion between the leaders of the Llano and the Nevada City colonies in which the latter suggested that the entire society be transferred to Nevada, but Harriman refused to consider that alternative.[26] He had long since come to view Eggleston and the socialists who had assisted in founding the Nevada organization as irresponsible and dishonest rivals.

During the summer of 1917, Jake Rhodes, an organizer

and opportunist, informed Harriman of a large tract of land in Louisiana belonging to the Gulf Lumber Company of St. Louis. A Texas real estate salesman soon arrived at Llano and as an agent for Gulf induced a committee to visit the Louisiana site. The company had cut the valuable pine timber, but after destruction of their sawmill by fire, they had left the hardwoods. In addition, many of the company's unpainted frame warehouses and other crude buildings remained. They could provide immediate housing for the colonists.

In early autumn, 1917, Harriman levied another mortgage on the California property, and a down payment of five thousand dollars was made on a nineteen-thousand-acre tract located southwest of Stables, Louisiana. The lumber company's headquarters and railway siding at Stables were two miles from Leesville, and eighteen miles east of the Sabine River. Although Stables, which was rechristened Newllano, had been deserted for only six months before the cadre of sixty-five adults arrived from California in late 1917, it had been stripped of electric wiring, water pipes, and all movables. The company directors soon found that they had contracted to pay $120,000 for a few primitive buildings and several thousand acres of sand, stumps, and swamps.

Gentry P. McCorkle was left in charge of the California colony, but within a year it had collapsed. Outside prosperity stimulated by the war, dejection after the exodus to Louisiana, inability to pay the lengthening list of creditors, and finally the refusal of McCorkle to pay cash wages led to the society's dissolution. McCorkle managed to secure the mortgage on much of the colony land, and as he forced the colonists out, he seized the property for himself.[27]

Technically, Newllano continued to maintain the old administrative and social forms of its California predecessor, but neither Harriman nor many of the other Llano leaders settled in Louisiana. Harriman divided his time between a legal battle with McCorkle, the securing of one thousand acres on the Isle of Pines, Cuba (where he contemplated a West Indian colony), and trying to regain his health in Brazil. In June, 1924, he was replaced as president of Newllano by George T. Pickett, and in October, 1925, he died of tuberculosis at his home in Los Angeles.

For twenty-two years the Llano del Rio Company of Nevada struggled in the humid forests of Louisiana. It was a pathetic anticlimax to the plans so feverishly undertaken in California. Newllano proved to be less the development of an idea than an idea in the process of disintegration. A series of fortuitous circumstances, however, allowed the colony to survive for more than two decades. The Gulf Lumber Company had no wish to foreclose its mortgage, and when the colony failed to meet its payments, Gulf merely executed a new and more liberal agreement. The catastrophe of depression drove many people to seek desperate remedies and to adopt overly sanguine attitudes in relation to mutual cooperatives. The colony tended to become a home for the old, the unemployed, and the ill. A further reason for Newllano's survival was the colony's unparalleled publication and advertising center. The inauguration of at least twelve newspapers and periodicals as well as the appearance of dozens of tracts and pamphlets made Newllano one of the best publicized socialist centers in the United States.

However, after George Pickett was literally driven from office in 1935, conditions deteriorated rapidly. Spies were used, violence erupted, immorality was charged, and finally in 1939, lawsuits terminated the colony's control of the property. But officially the Llano del Rio Company of Nevada did not die. It continued to file an annual list of officers and directors, pay the necessary fees, and maintain a resident agent in Nevada. The most recent meeting of the board of directors was called in Reno in October, 1962.

EVALUATION

Repelled by the pattern of prewar life, Job Harriman attempted to organize a faceless, but efficient, society which, if successful, would have been anything but utopian. He argued, in effect, that perfect freedom in a cooperative colony would result in the participants not wanting to be truly free, but adhering, rather, to a sort of communal oversoul. Ultimately, there was to be no selfishness, and only the welfare of the community would count. There would be cooperation, but no competition, no struggle for wealth or status, and no social mobility because each person would accept the position assigned to him. Docility rather than freedom would be the rule. By making a socialist robot of himself, the colonist could escape the pain of being a man or a citizen. The leaders believed that through the use of education, observation, and training, mankind could be conditioned to behave in a cooperative manner and in time automatically and harmoniously respond to the needs of the community.

But Harriman, himself, was one of the first to admit that the appeal to reason had been misdirected and that true "socialism played a very small part" in the behavior of the colonists.[28] "We had imagined that men who believed in socialism would react more or less alike to the same environment. . . ." But they acted "as differently as they would have acted had they never heard of socialism." Neither did the cooperative environment alter their course very much. In fact, "the selfish persisted in their course with a persistence that was amazing." Harriman was also surprised to find "that there were more selfish men among the poor, in proportion to their number, than there were among the well-to-do." Even more disturbing was the breakdown of the Marxian doctrine and the deterministic theory of life upon which the entire project was grounded. "After three years' observation some of us were convinced that the materialistic philosophy, including economic determinism, was not sufficient to explain the phenomena that were going on about us." Finally, Harriman concluded that while man reacted to his environment there was in addition a "potential energy" and "driving force" which was "determined by the quality of one's emotions and feelings." An inner force molded man's attitude toward society rather than vice versa.

Although the Nevada colony was a historical, philosophical, and administrative offshoot of Job Harriman's Llano, its leaders were always men more of action than of analysis. In Llano, a doctrine failed; at Nevada City, a movement failed. Harriman was a prophet who pointed the way; Eggleston was a salesman who carried a message into the marketplace. The Nevada society reflected the difference. Rather than being situated in a desert, it was located in a well-watered valley; rather than attempting to tame wild lands, it secured prosperous ranches; rather than ignoring politics, it was founded for political action; rather than creating animosity among outsiders, it was generally welcomed by the community; rather than requiring a somewhat rigid social pattern, it allowed considerable personal independence. The leaders at Nevada City were never very serious about digging to the roots of man's needs; instead, they attempted to appeal to his emotions and direct his behavior.

NOTES

[1] A. B. Forbes, "The Literary Quest for Utopia, 1880–90," *Social Forces*, VI (December, 1927), 182.

[2] Patricia M. Bauer, "Cooperative Colonies in California" (A bibliography collected from printed and manuscript material located in the Bancroft Library, Berkeley, California).

[3] Robert V. Hine, *California's Utopian Colonies* (San Marino: the Huntington Library, 1953), p. 114.

[4] Ernest S. Wooster, *Communities of the Past and Present* (Newllano: Llano Co-Operative Colony, 1924), p. 120.

[5] Willoughby Rodman, *The History of the Bench and Bar of Southern California* (Los Angeles: William J. Porter, 1909), p. 170.

[6] George E. Mowry, *The California Progressives* (Berkeley: University of California Press, 1951). The study offers an excellent discussion of the economic recession of 1913 and the part played by both Harriman and the Progressive party in Los Angeles politics.

[7] The romantic view seems to have originated with an article in the colony publication *The Gateway to Freedom* (Los Angeles: Colony Press Department, 1914).

[8] James A. McDonald, *The Llano Co-Operative Colony and What It Taught* (San Antonio: Carleton Printing Company, 1950), p. 15.

[9] For an example of the transfer of land see Office of the Recorder, Los Angeles County, Grantee Book 6005 (February 19, 1915), p. 56. For a firsthand account of the financial structure of the colony see the unpubl. thesis (University of Southern California, 1918) by Archie Roy Clifton, "A study of Llano del Rio Community in the Light of Earlier Experiments in Practical Socialism."

[10] Clifton, *op. cit.*, p. 32.

[11] *Ibid.*, p. 64.

[12] *Western Comrade* (Llano), April, 1916, see article "The Gateway to Freedom."

[13] Robert Brown, *Can We Co-Operate?* (Pleasant Plains, New York: Roving Eye Press, 1940), p. 215.

[14] Much confusion has surrounded the chartering of the corporation in Nevada. One of the more fanciful stories was told by the

colony physician, R. K. Williams. According to Williams, a meeting was called to read the commissioner's report to the colonists. From 7:00 P.M. until 3:30 A.M. Harriman, although sick with tuberculosis, answered the acrimonious and belligerent charges of the colonists. After the threatening meeting he and a few friends jumped into his big black automobile and drove to Carson City where early the following morning, after a private discussion with a local judge, the company was incorporated in Nevada. See the unpubl. thesis (Tulane University, 1936) by Fred Hanover, "Llano Cooperative Colony: An American Rural Community Experiment," pp. 55–56.

[15] *Western Comrade*, April, 1915, see back cover.

[16] Interview with Artie Riggle, Sparks, Nevada, November 24, 1962.

[17] C. V. Eggleston to L. V. Flowers, March 6, 1917, in Miscellaneous No. 9 of the McCarran Papers in the Nevada Historical Society, Reno.

[18] See Nevada Colony Corporation, Office of the Secretary of State, Carson City, Nevada.

[19] *Nevada State Journal* (Reno), February 11, 1916, p. 8, c. 3.

[20] *Nevada State Journal*, December 30, 1915, p. 4, c. 4; February 13, 1916, p. 5, c. 6; February 26, 1916, p. 3, c. 5; February 27, 1916, p. 6, c. 1.

[21] During February and early March, 1916, the Llano del Rio Company of California secured depositions from holders of more than two-thirds of the 369,037 shares of stock authorizing the sale. See Llano del Rio Company, Office of the Recorder, Los Angeles County, California.

[22] Llano del Rio Company of Nevada, Office of the Secretary of State, Carson City, Nevada.

[23] E. G. Eggleston to C. W. McDade, March 12, 1917, in Miscellaneous No. 8 of the McCarran Papers.

[24] In Miscellaneous No. 6 of the McCarran Papers.

[25] The Llano Company's original title to the land was brought into question when a suit was filed by the Southern Pacific Land Company. Office of the Recorder, Los Angeles County, Grantor Book 6668 (May 10, 1918), p. 175.

[26] R. E. Bray to Samuel J. Taylor, February 15, 1918, and June 12, 1918, in Miscellaneous No. 3 of the McCarran Papers.

[27] Office of the Recorder, Los Angeles County, Grantor Book 6793 (April 23, 1919), p. 195.

[28] Wooster, *op. cit.* (see n. 4 above), see Harriman's introduction.

Cooperative Socialism
and the
Nevada Appeal

AT FIRST, Nevada City was the outgrowth of the legal problems faced by the Llano colony. As conceived by Job Harriman, the Nevada operation was to have been a relatively insignificant facet of the California organization, created solely to facilitate incorporation under Nevada law. But C. V. Eggleston quickly sensed that the socialistic and cooperative potential of the community lay much deeper. He believed that the idea of a cooperative commonwealth in the American West could be readily fitted into the Churchill County environment. Eggleston argued that the cooperative appeal of socialism, as first set forth by Laurence Gronlund in 1884, could be grafted onto Nevada radicalism.

THE BROTHERHOOD OF THE CO-OPERATIVE COMMONWEALTH

The most meaningful single antecedent in shaping the Nevada experiment was Laurence Gronlund's *The Co-operative Commonwealth*, published in 1884. With the breakup of the Edward Bellamy cooperative clubs about 1890, the works of the Danish-born Gronlund began to attract wide acceptance. In a reasoned and simplified analysis of Marxism, Gronlund argued that socialism could be achieved through the creation of small, economically self-sufficient colonies which would eventually increase in size and number until the cooperative socialists could gain political control of the state. Several leading socialists worked for the inclusion of the Gronlund program into the People's party platform of the early 1890's, but the idea was generally ignored by the populists.

A few colonies of the period, like the Christian Commonwealth in Georgia, the Ruskin Cooperative in Tennessee, and Kaweah in California, borrowed heavily from the Gronlund program, but all were politically ineffectual and short-lived. However, in the autumn of 1895, a Maine reformer suggested in scores of letters to socialists that all cooperatives in the United States be drawn together into one vast fraternal organization. The following summer Eugene Debs, a professed Gronlundite, and other labor leaders called a convention in which they implemented the Maine proposal by founding the Brotherhood of the Co-operative Commonwealth. The organization determined to establish a cooperative colony in some western state, supervise a mass migration, and thereby provide at least token relief for the unemployed. The organizers saw the movement not only as a relief for victims of capitalism and a method by which to unify all cooperatives, but also as a device for gaining political control in the western United States. The colonists in the sparsely populated state would nominate candidates for political office and capture the state government, thus providing a base from which cooperative socialism could expand in all directions.[1] The idea received surprisingly enthusiastic support even from seasoned union leaders. Projects were considered in Colorado and Tennessee, and two feeble attempts were made to establish colonies in Washington.[2] Eggleston's later plans for the Nevada society were merely a leaf from the 1896 and 1897 program of the Brotherhood of the Co-operative Commonwealth.

In June, 1897, the American Railway Union, seriously weakened by the Pullman strike, met in Chicago and formed the Social Democracy of America. Many leaders of the new social action group were members of one of the 125 branches of the Brotherhood of the Co-operative Commonwealth; therefore, they emphasized the establishment of western colonies. At the close of the conference, Debs wrote John D. Rockefeller and others asking for assistance in the creation of colonies where both "millionaires and beggars" would disappear. But only $2,421 was collected for the cooperatives, and eastern critics of the program declared: "People cannot be kept enthusiastic in 44 states over the prospect of establishing a model commonwealth in the 45th on easy payments."[3]

By the time of the second party convention in June, 1898, a deep split had developed over the colony idea; nevertheless, when the issue was brought to a vote, the colonization forces, urged on by Emma Goldman, defeated the political activists fifty-two to thirty-seven. At that point, forces supporting political action bolted the convention, conducted their own conference, and formed the Social Democratic party. Although in a majority at the June convention, the cooperators, with their plans to capture the nation through western colonies, quickly melted away. Most of their membership drifted over into the Social Democratic party. In

March, 1900, the Harriman or "Kangaroo" faction of the Social Labor party also joined the Social Democrats. In 1901, the Social Democratic party reorganized and became the American Socialist party.

Although dormant for almost two decades, the ideas of the cooperative commonwealth were not forgotten. When the Socialist party became engulfed in the confusion surrounding World War I, C. V. Eggleston emerged as a prophet anxious to lead the people back to the firm cooperative doctrines of the 1890's. Therefore, in his own way Eggleston presented a broader and more ambitious plan than Harriman. He quickly aroused support for the program in the West, and among midwestern socialists who had been members of the Brotherhood of the Co-operative Commonwealth, he received an enthusiastic reception.

But in the final analysis, neither the legal accident of corporation laws nor the theoretical beliefs of Eggleston would have been sufficient to create the Fallon experiment had not Nevada's historical development, peculiar population trends, and federal irrigation projects prepared the way for the venture into cooperative socialism.

RELIGIOUS AND ETHNIC COLONIES OF NEVADA

In many ways the ideas of community planning and cooperative control stressed by both Harriman and Eggleston were not new to the state of Nevada. The early Mormon settlers, particularly in the eastern and southern parts of the state, had found it necessary to work together during the first difficult years. At Bunkerville, on the left bank of the Virgin River, a communal society functioned under a special arrangement with the church. Edward Bunker, Sr., led a party of twenty-three families from Santa Clara, Utah, to a location just south of the river during the late 1870's; the advance party of six wagons and seventy head of cattle arrived on January 5, 1877. In addition to the general directives of the church, the United Order had been formulated "wherein every person contributed according to his capacity, shared according to his needs, and participated in mutual ownership and management of all community properties."[4] As the community hall, common kitchen, houses of willow saplings, and an irrigation system were completed, the party became confident that they could form a completely self-sufficient society. Chores were done on a rotation schedule so that there would be no occasion for charges of discrimination or jealousy. Crops of cotton, wheat, corn, vegetables, and cane were grown, and all products placed in a central storehouse for the use of everyone. Within two years, however, the communal system resulted in serious disagreements, and steps were taken to relax the community controls. In 1881, the United Order was dissolved and the property divided among the participants.[5]

Although differing from the United Order, the Nevada Land and Livestock Company contributed significantly to Mormon colonization at the turn of the century. Typical of the company's activities was the purchase of the McQuitty ranch near Ely and the establishment of the Georgetown colony. The 560 acres were subdivided into plots of about ten acres each and the water of Murray Creek used for irrigation. The experiment was short-lived, however, because in July, 1902, the twenty-nine families comprising the colony sold the entire property to the New York and Nevada Copper Company for $35,000. In the same period, the church purchased numerous ranches along the White River in White Pine and Nye counties, divided them into small farms, established townsites, and supervised the formation of many eastern Nevada communities.[6]

In the two decades before World War I, several religious and communal organizations inspected Nevada's remote valleys in search of a Shangri-la which could easily be converted into a productive and self-sufficient paradise. During the spring and summer of 1904, the Dunkards studied Lemmon Valley and Spanish Springs in Washoe County with a view to moving their entire Muncie, Indiana, congregation. But after a visit by their astute leader, Elder George L. Studebaker of the famous wagon-automobile family, the location was ruled inadequate for their needs.[7] The House of David, organized in 1903 at Benton Harbor, Michigan, declared that Rhyolite, Nevada, was to be a Mecca where members of the "lost tribes of Israel" could reassemble. According to the House of David, 144,000 persons were to be drawn together before the millenium would come, so southern Nevada was slated to become the scene for much immigration and conversion. D. K. Eubanks, leader of the Nevada contingent, had worked as a miner in the state before he drifted to Michigan and with conversion discovered that he was a descendent of the lost tribe. He thereupon returned to Nevada to preach communalism, vegetarianism, and chastity and, with a party of five elders, to lay plans for the Rhyolite colony.[8]

Occasionally, a group of wanderers actually fashioned their Nevada Elysium. In June, 1897, the 5,500-acre Wymore ranch in Smith Valley was offered for sale. On August 12, Ephraim Deinard, secretary of the Hebrew Agricultural Society of the United States, wrote to Nevada's German-born governor, Reinhold Sadler, requesting "encouragement and moral assistance."[9] The society had been organized in Philadelphia in 1891 for the purpose of helping Russian and Polish Jews to colonize. Jewish philanthropists had financed the settlement of small parties in many parts of the United States as well as in Canada and South America, but the colonies had collapsed, and some twelve hundred Jewish peasants had drifted into Philadelphia. On July 1, 1897, the society moved to San Francisco, but after failing to find suitable locations for most of its unemployed farmers in California, decided to locate in Nevada.[10]

Governor Sadler informed T. R. Hofer and Morris Cohn, local promoters from Carson City, of the Jewish plight. The two men grasped their opportunity by tentatively purchasing the Wymore property in Smith Valley, then hurrying to San Francisco where, in late October, they signed an agreement to settle an initial cadre of seventeen families on the new site.[11] By late November, 1897, twenty-five families had made their way to the Lyon County tract. Finding that Hofer and Cohn had failed to complete the purchase of the land, they finally gained permission to settle by dealing directly with Wymore.[12] In August, 1898, the president and the secretary of the colony mortgaged the community's crop at a Carson City bank, then fled to Philadelphia with the funds.[13] By December, 1898, the Hebrew Benevolent Society of San Francisco was financing the movement of the colonists back to California.

Many of the immigrants had previously attempted colony life in North Dakota, others had failed in Canada's Northwest Territory, and still others had worked together in a communal undertaking at Porterville, California. Drouth in Dakota, an unfavorable climate in Canada, dissension in California, and mismanagement at all three locations had resulted in the collapse of the experiments. At Wellington, Nevada, the group was plagued by most of the former problems plus the dishonesty of their leaders, an aversion to farm labor, and a shortage of water for irrigation.[14] The thousands of Russian, Polish, German, and Austrian Jews that were to make Smith Valley into the new Israel never arrived, and Nevada failed to "triple in population in the next five years."[15] Nor was the state's symbol of silver immediately replaced by an emblem embossed with vegetables as had been promised by the overly exuberant local press.

The Mormons at Bunkerville, Orthodox Jews in Smith Valley, and the flirtative activities of the Dunkards, the House of David, German parties in Elko County, and Hungarians from New York City typify the problems faced by the primitive, the poor, the religious, and the ethnic groups who wished to form cooperative communities in Nevada. But Nevada was changing, and the older and more simplified religious cooperatives tended to be overshadowed by more pressing and pragmatic colonization.

NEVADA'S PROGRAMS FOR LAND SETTLEMENT

To understand the generally favorable reception given to Fallon socialism, it is important to recall that for more than two decades after 1880, Nevadans were prodded by harsh reality and pricked by economic necessity. They thereby became realists and opportunists ready to blend outside doctrine into their homemade philosophy to relieve homely ills. Jacksonianism still lingered on the frontier, but it had been tinged with a current and purposeful radicalism.

According to the census of 1900, Nevada was the only state to suffer a loss in population. Whereas the seven other intermountain states enjoyed a population increase of approximately threefold between 1880 and 1900, Nevada experienced a decrease of one third. The mines had steadily declined from their peak production of the late 1870's, and the income from agriculture and livestock had undergone a downward trend. Neither the official launching of a state agricultural society in 1885 nor the creation of a state immigration bureau in 1887 stimulated settlement within the state.[16] The suggestions by Senator William Stewart that colonies should be organized in eastern cities to settle on western lands was idle oratory,[17] and the repeated demands of Senator John P. Jones and the Nevada Cattlemen's Association that the federal government transfer public lands to the state for agricultural colonization were unsound economics.[18] With its decline in population, the state faced serious tax problems and was in no position to finance the construction of the dams and canals necessary to stimulate agricultural settlement. The Jones theory was popular during the late 1880's, however. A Carson City paper suggested that with the cession of land to the state, a hundred thousand people would inhabit the Carson River basin. "In less than five years bells on top of school houses, churches, public halls, gardens and libraries would be within the sound of each other's voice from Genoa to Ragtown [*sic*]."[19]

Perhaps the most active Nevada organization in the field of immigration and group settlement was the State Board of Trade organized by Francis G. Newlands in late 1889. The unofficial body grew from the Washoe Improvement Association; through the diplomatic handling of Newlands it gained the active support of Governor Charles C. Stevenson, Senator William Stewart, the Central Pacific Railroad, and most business and government leaders.[20] The board worked with private citizens and local organizations in encouraging rural settlement. Railroads, including the Central Pacific and the Virginia and Truckee, offered special rates to settlers, and the *Reno Weekly Gazette* provided free tickets for agents representing groups of interested colonists. In the early 1890's, parties of prospective migrants were contacted throughout the United States and urged to visit Nevada. On one occasion, representatives for one hundred Tennessee families were finally induced by the secretary of the board to inspect the lands near Reno, but the first morning after their arrival, an unseasonal September snowstorm ended the negotiations.[21]

With the failure of community immigration programs and the unlikelihood of a liberal cession of land by the central government, Newlands joined in the drive to secure direct federal assistance for irrigation and reclamation projects. Of course, national involvement in the administration and settling of land was not a new idea. The Homestead Act of 1862, with its provisions for the granting of 160 acres to each homesteader, was designed with the compact and productive lands of the East in mind. It offered few inducements for settlers on the western ranges. The Desert Land Act of 1877, applicable only in the West, was the congressional attempt to give balance to the 1862 act. The law allowed for the purchase of 640 acres at $1.25 per acre, but included the absurd stipulation that the entire section must be irrigated within three years after filing. Although subsequent modifications were enacted, the measure remained essentially useless and inoperative. In 1894, in the Carey Act, Congress made a further attempt to stimulate settlement on western land. Subject to certain federal regulations, one million acres could be granted to each of the eight arid-land states. The purpose was to allow and encourage the states to undertake irrigation and reclamation projects. In 1908, the eight states were granted an additional million acres apiece, but they did not respond, and the experiment proved a failure.[22]

Agitation in the West had led in 1891 to the founding of the National Irrigation Congress as an annual forum where the public land policy and irrigation and reclamation needs could be reviewed. The group moved steadily toward greater federal involvement. J. E. Stubbs, president of the University of Nevada, was appointed one of the state's delegates to the conference in 1899. As chairman of the Committee on Resolutions he introduced a motion demanding "the construction by the federal government of storage reservoirs and irrigation works wherever necessary. . . ." Furthermore, water from all streams should remain public property, and public lands should be held by the federal government and not ceded to the states. The conference passed the Stubbs resolution unanimously.[23]

During the 1890's most Nevadans became convinced that the state had been drained of its wealth, exploited by outsiders, and neglected by the government. Its bullion had helped to preserve the Union, and its gold and silver had built metropolitan centers outside its borders. Nevadans felt that the national government should redress the wrongs by reclaiming the land and providing a stimulus to immigration and colonization. The growing protest was reflected in the state's politics. During the decade the Prohibition party, the Peoples' party, the Silver party, the Stalwart-Silver party, the Silver-Democratic Alliance, and somewhat later the Progressives all sought and gained considerable recognition. Nevada led the nation in its support of James B.

Weaver for President in 1892; the Populist-Silver party received two and a half times as many votes as the Republicans and Democrats combined. In 1896, when Congressman Newlands, as a Silver-Democrat, called for federal action to nationalize mines, rivers, and public utilities, he defeated his Republican opponent five to one.

Even the Republican *Reno Evening Gazette* supported federal action. After the accession of Theodore Roosevelt in 1901, it declared: "If President Roosevelt takes the stand for irrigation that it is believed he will it will double the population of Nevada before his term of office expires. Double—did we say—it will triple, and quadruple it, and those who have been hanging on in Nevada through the years of her decadence, will be glad they didn't have money to get away."[24] Nevada did not have long to wait. The Federal Reclamation Act authored by Francis G. Newlands became law in 1902 and for the first time carried the national government into the reclamation business.

THE NEWLANDS COLONIZATION ERA

The Newlands Act provided that all money received from the "sale and dispatch" of public lands in thirteen western states and three territories, except moneys for educational purposes, should be set aside in a reclamation fund. The money was to be used for examination, survey, construction, and maintenance of irrigation works, and for the storage and diversion of water. In 1902-1903, Newlands' influence in the Nevada legislature not only won his election to the United States Senate, it also secured the passage of a law which provided for the cooperation of the state of Nevada in a broad federal reclamation program. In the autumn of 1903, work on the Truckee-Carson project was commenced, and Nevada became the first state to construct irrigation works under the new legislation.

A diversion dam was erected near Derby on the Truckee River, and a canal thirty-three miles long carried water to the Carson River. By September, 1910, the government had expended four million dollars and had contracted to irrigate 90,703 acres of land. In accordance with the original plans, the construction of a storage reservoir on the lower Carson River was started in 1911. Lahonton Dam was completed in 1915. Ninety percent of the land brought under cultivation by the Truckee-Carson project was in Churchill County.[25]

As one of the eight original counties, Churchill lay astride two of the early emigrant roads. The flatlands of the lower Carson River invited irrigation, and the first ditches and drainage canals had been dug in 1862. In the early years, much of the wild hay was cut and hauled to Virginia City. Later, cattle were driven in from as far as Oregon for fattening in the Stillwater district, and drovers from central Nevada used the valley as a resting and feeding area on their way to the rail shipping point at Wadsworth. Nevertheless, Churchill was the slowest growing county in the state. It had fewer than 500 persons in 1880, and only 830 by 1900.

After 1903, the agricultural population of the Lahonton Valley grew rapidly from some 72 families in 1905 to 400 families in 1908 to 469 families by 1911. The population of Churchill County grew from 830 in 1900 to 2,811 in 1910. The Fallon post office dated from the late 1890's, but the town was not officially designated the seat of Churchill County until 1902, and not incorporated until 1909. A municipally organized water, light, and power company was completed in 1912, and neither the public-owned utility plant nor the community owned and operated telephone system met with capitalistic opposition.

Obviously the Truckee-Carson project was to attract national and even international attention, and during twelve years of construction, the many colonization plans as well as the agricultural potential of the area received exaggerated newspaper coverage. Articles explaining that fifty thousand people were to locate in the valley were mere fantasy, whereas headlines declaring "The Colonization of Nevada Has Begun in Earnest" and "Colonization Association Buys Much Good Land" and "Colonists on the Way" reflect journalistic overstatement. Reports circulated in 1905 claimed that "several thousand Norwegian families from Minnesota and the Dakotas" were soon to arrive in western Nevada.[26] Colonization associations were formed for the purpose of clearing large tracts of land, securing water rights, and subdividing and selling the plots to settlers at a substantial profit.

Everyone seemed enamored of the term colonization. Land was the one commodity Nevada had in abundance, and only through its utilization could the state prosper. In 1911, the Ormsby County Development and Colonization Association was organized to finance the purchase of land and settle colonists along the Carson River. Although generally unsuccessful, similar movements followed. In 1915, even Henry Ford agreed to discuss Nevada's problems, and Judge W. W. Griffin traveled to San Francisco to meet the industrialist. Local boosters were certain that a great tide of immigrants would soon be pouring into western Nevada.[27]

In 1916, Washoe County promoters announced the formation of a boys' town with facilities for five thousand youths between the ages of twelve and eighteen. The new facility on the Truckee River was to provide the old lumbering town of Verdi with a new lease on life.[28] The Reno Commercial Club contributed to the immigration movement by furnishing information for prospective settlers and publishing lengthy lists of persons interested in migrating to the area. In late 1916, as Eggleston was advertising the Fallon colony, Ramsey M. Cox, general manager of the Nevada, California and Oregon Railway, asked that the Nevada legislature establish an immigration board to procure and "care for" immigrants. Long-term loans, easy payments for land, and even direct financial aid was urged by the railroad official. Cox emphasized that the settlement of the land for one hundred miles around Reno was an urgent necessity and that every new migrant was worth one thousand dollars to the city.[29]

Promotion of Nevada colonies was not limited to the newly reclaimed land, and although most projects were stillborn, a few communities temporarily blossomed into major centers of activity. The town of Metropolis, in Elko County, was an outgrowth of the colonization craze and the Pacific Reclamation Company's ambitious and well-planned publicity program. The town, located some twelve miles northwest of Wells, flourished while the hotel, railroad station, and paved streets were being constructed, and by early 1912 represented a community of ninety-three families. Although not organized as a communal venture, common needs and problems led to communitywide action and the creation of a cooperative buying and marketing system. But despite the claims of the *Metropolis Chronicle*, promotional brochures, and experienced land salesmen, there were not fourteen inches of rain per year, and the dam in Immigrant Canyon could not provide water to irrigate thirty-three thousand acres of agricultural land. The project collapsed with the town only partly completed, and Americans, Canadians, and Europeans who had envisioned a life of genteel prosperity on the fertile plains quickly abandoned Lincoln School and Madison Park to the drifting sand, the sagebrush, and the jackrabbits.[30]

The long decades of decline brought the people of Nevada to favor both cooperative and governmental action and to support almost any plan that promised immigration to the state. The Truckee-Carson project stimulated the colonization boom and, concurrently, the discovery and development of minerals in southern and eastern Nevada fostered radical labor and militant socialism. Thus, the three needs for the Fallon experiment were joined: a friendly populace, government-watered land, and an active Socialist party.

SOCIALISM IN NEVADA

During the first five years of the twentieth century, large mining operations were undertaken at Tonopah, Goldfield, Rhyolite, Manhattan, and Ely. Tens of thousands of miners poured into the state. The new methods of industrial monopoly and organized labor caused a series of bitter disputes. The results were quickly obvious. A socialist organization which first entered Nevada politics in the election of 1904, reorganized in July, 1908, and almost tripled its vote. Indeed, the national convention of a socialist splinter group, the Labor-Socialist party, met in New York City in July, 1908, and chose M. W. Preston, an inmate of the Nevada

State Prison, as their presidential candidate. Preston had become nationally famous when he was convicted for murder during the labor trouble in Goldfield in 1907.[31]

In November, 1908, Nevada's socialist contender for United States Senator received 1,939 votes; 12,473 votes went to the victorious Democratic candidate. In 1910, the top socialist vote was increased to 3,639, but more significant, the national organization became convinced that Nevada could be carried for the party.[32] Before the election of 1912, a dozen socialist speakers of national reputation campaigned throughout the state, and 200,000 pieces of socialist literature were distributed.[33] Their efforts were rewarded. With M. J. Scanlan's election in Nye County, Nevada could claim one of the three socialist state senators in the United States. Socialist I. F. Davis represented Nye County in the Assembly. Only six states other than Nevada had socialists seated in the lower house of the legislature. Twenty-nine county and township offices in Nevada were also filled by socialists.[34] In the 1914 election for United States Senator, Francis G. Newlands, the organizer of Nevada's reclamation projects, received 8,078 votes to socialist A. Grant Miller's 5,451, and conditions seemed propitious for a socialist victory in 1916. C. V. Eggleston was soon to put forward the Nevada Colony Corporation as an instrument for securing "five thousand new Socialist votes" which would "change the state to Socialism." Local party officials were inclined to agree when he concluded, "Where is there anything in all the world so full of hope and promise as this plan!"[35]

In the meantime a significant geographical and occupational shift was occurring in Nevada socialism. Although the party had gained its first strength in the mining communities, the predominantly agricultural Churchill County grew rapidly as a socialist center. In April, 1911, a socialist group in Fallon headed by Dr. John E. Warden and Fred C. Sander launched the *Ballot Box* with the caption, "Workers of the world unite at the Ballot Box. You have nothing to lose but your chains and a world to gain." Although a four-page weekly, the publication devoted only the first two or three columns on page one to Churchill County and Nevada news. The remainder was national news and standard socialist filler. The paper was printed at a central plant in Iola, Kansas, which by early 1913 was issuing fifty-nine similar journals. Fifteen of the papers were for distribution in Texas, ten in Oklahoma, six in Arkansas, and seven in Kansas. The plant published one paper for Colorado, but only the *Ballot Box* was published for the region west of the Rocky Mountains. Since most of the publications were circulated in the Midwest and Southwest, much of the material dealt with that region. Oklahoma received special attention. With fifty-eight out of seventy-seven counties holding regular socialist conventions, Oklahoma claimed the most widespread organization of any state. The *Ballot Box*, therefore, tended to create a political tie between the Kansas and Oklahoma socialists and the Fallon community. It was a relationship which proved significant in the settlement of Nevada City.

The Fallon paper gave extended coverage to Job Harriman's campaign for mayor of Los Angeles and his defense of the McNamara brothers. When the McNamaras confessed their guilt, the journal, like all socialist publications, reflected shock but explained the action by declaring that capitalism "breeds slaves, cowards and criminals."[36] In the publication's suggested list of good books, either Karl Marx or Friedrich Engels was author of the first six. Particular attention was focused on Marx and his theories. "He agitated, organized and instructed. He sent his disciples into every civilized country where, little by little, they built up tremendous organizations of labor."[37] On July 8, 1911, the entire paper was printed with red ink to signify the close association between American Independence and Marxian doctrine. On November 4, an article entitled "Why We See Red" began with the sentence, "That's the color, red, r-e-d, RED."[38]

Throughout the period, key socialist leaders spoke at Reno, Tonopah, and Fallon. Fallon prided itself on being able to assure any socialist dignitary an audience of at least 275 voters. The local met on the first and third Sundays with a picnic or basket dinner usually accompanying the first Sunday meeting. Sunday excursions on a chartered locomotive to Lahonton Dam provided additional excitement. During the spring of 1912, the party was particularly active; it gained about ten new members a month, and in March, 1912, twenty-seven new voters were enlisted in the cause. By May 5 the Churchill group had 119 members and thereby claimed the largest number of registered socialists per total vote cast (817 in 1910) of any county in the United States.[39] Indeed, by May, 1912, Churchill County had twelve more bonafide socialists than the entire state of Nevada had had in 1910.

With the announcement in 1912 that Job Harriman was traveling to Churchill County to speak for the party and that the vice-presidential nominee planned to make Tonopah and Fallon two of his last major stops before the November election, the Fallon editor reflected understandable pride. He emphasized that Churchill socialists enjoyed many distinctions. They had one of the largest organizations in the country, perhaps the liveliest and fastest growing party, and also the most congenial group. Only two members had withdrawn from the Fallon local. Furthermore, Churchill had made a larger financial contribution to the party than any other county in the state. Nor was the process of becoming a socialist a mere formality. Careful scrutiny was given to applications, and in addition to local, state, and national dues, there was a campaign assessment of twenty-five cents per month designed to pay the one-hundred-dollar filing fee required of candidates by Nevada law. The *Ballot Box* concluded that "Socialists for whom Socialism is more than a political party program, for whom Socialism is a philosophy of life and a system of ethics, are idealists and prophets. They lift the rank and file of the Socialist Party above the small matters of every day vegetation and inspire them with a motive and greater activity."[40] Many Fallon socialists were ideologically ready for the colonization doctrines of Job Harriman and sufficiently motivated to accept the salesmanship of C. V. Eggleston.

Although the *Ballot Box* widely publicized the candidates for county and township offices, the election of 1912 proved somewhat disappointing. The socialist vote of 212 in Churchill County indicated that few nonparty members supported the socialist ticket. Nevertheless, it was a marked gain over the 53 socialist votes of 1908 and the 119—for governor—in 1910.[41] In the spring of 1913, a Lyceum was organized at Fallon, and leading socialist speakers visited the Lahonton Valley on their national circuit. Discontinuance of the *Ballot Box* on June 21, 1913, was to some extent offset by the inauguration of the *Nevada Socialist* in Reno in mid-1914. The new party paper gave special notice to the activities of Churchill County, where two new socialist locals were founded, and representatives were seated on every election board by November, 1914. Although local socialist candidates were again defeated in 1914, many were ready to dedicate themselves to the more demanding venture soon to be launched at Nevada City.

It was unusual that one of the largest and most vital socialist groups in the state developed in the newest and most rapidly growing agricultural district. But news of the first federal reclamation undertaking had spread throughout the country, and even immigrants from Europe were drawn to Nevada by foreign language leaflets describing the project.[42] As a result of the boom psychology and the expanding opportunities of the district, hundreds of families arrived who were inexperienced and temperamentally ill-equipped for farming. Many were in search of something for nothing; most tried to farm before sufficient water became available; some homesteaded lands that could never be cultivated; few possessed sufficient capital to develop their land; and others cleared the brush only to have the soil blow away.[43] As dissatisfaction mounted, many political leaders demanded that the government provide direct and immediate assistance. In the campaign for United States Senator in 1914, the Republican Samuel Platt came forward with the suggestion that land and water were not enough. The federal government must advance credit for the ditching, clearing, and leveling of the land; for the construction of buildings; and for the purchase of machinery, tools, and seed. As the author of America's reclamation program, Newlands carried the state, but he defeated Platt and his progressive platform by only forty votes. By 1914, therefore, the Republican, the Democratic, and the Socialist candidates for the Senate had all come to support greater governmental involvement with community problems.[44]

As Churchill County grew and settlers rushed in, the early harmony within the Fallon socialist locals was replaced by disagreements and dissension. Both the rough and the radical elements became more vocal; harangues replaced analysis at party meetings, and mortgages fostered demands for more direct action. Thoughtful socialists reflected the discontent by suggesting not only greater cooperation between government and farmer, but also greater cooperation between farmer and farmer. The cooperators wished to experiment, discuss, and administer together. They believed that individualistic capitalism had broken down the values of yesterday and that only cooperative socialism could provide the truths of tomorrow. The local Fallon ranchers who gave their land to found a colony somehow hoped to arrive at a great socialist reality through the formation of a small cooperative community.

NOTES

[1] Ray Ginger, *Eugene V. Debs: A Biography* (New York: Collier Books, 1962), pp. 172, 209.

[2] Howard H. Quint, *The Forging of American Socialism* (New York: Bobbs-Merrill Company, Inc., 1964), pp. 305, 318.

[3] Ginger, *op. cit.*, p. 211.

[4] *Nevada: A Guide to the Silver State* (Portland, Ore.: Binfords and Mort, 1940), p. 180.

[5] Francis E. Leavitt, "The Influence of the Mormon People in the Settlement of Clark County" (unpubl. thesis, University of Nevada, 1934), pp. 123–141.

[6] *White Pine News* (Ely), July 3, 1902, p. 1, c. 5 and July 31, 1902, p. 1, c. 5; *Reno Evening Gazette*, July 31, 1905, p. 5, c. 4.

[7] *Reno Evening Gazette*, August 11, 1904, p. 5, cc. 1–2.

[8] *Reno Evening Gazette*, June 12, 1907, p. 6, c. 3.

[9] *Letter Box 25981.* "Letters to and from the Governor's Office, 1897–1899." Nevada Historical Society, Reno.

[10] *Ibid.* See printed circular "The Colonization Question of Russian Jews in America."

[11] *Yerington Rustler*, October 28, 1897, p. 4, c. 2.

[12] For a lengthy and colorful description of the arrival of the colonists see the Doten Diaries, University of Nevada library, Vol. 73, entry of November 9, 1897.

[13] *Reno Weekly Gazette*, August 11, 1898, p. 2, c. 4 and September 15, 1898, p. 3, c. 3.

[14] *Reno Weekly Gazette*, November 11, 1897, p. 7, c. 3; *Gardnerville Record*, September 13, 1898, p. 2, c. 3.

[15] *Reno Weekly Gazette*, November 25, 1897, p. 1, c. 5.

[16] *Statutes of the State of Nevada*, Passed at the Thirteenth Session of the Legislature, 1887 (Carson City: State Printing Office, 1897), pp. 90–91.

[17] *Weekly Gazette and Stockman* (Reno), May 16, 1889, p. 8, c. 2.

[18] *Carson Free Lance*, May 11, 1885, p. 4, c. 2 and March 29, 1886, p. 1, c. 1.

[19] *Morning Appeal* (Carson City), January 30, 1887, p. 2, c. 1.

[20] *History of the Organization of the Nevada State Board of Trade* (Reno: Gazette Steam Book and Job Print, 1890).

[21] *Reno Weekly Gazette*, November 11, 1897, p. 7, c. 3.

[22] By June 30, 1934, only 1,102,586 acres of western land had been transferred to private owners under the Carey Act, and much of this had not been brought under irrigation.

[23] *Daily Independent* (Elko), October 3, 1899, p. 2, c. 1.

[24] *Reno Evening Gazette*, November 15, 1901, p. 2, c. 1.

[25] *Reclaimed Nevada: The Truckee-Carson Project*, Bulletin, circulated by the Nevada State Bureau of Industry, Agriculture and Irrigation (Reno: Nevada State Journal Print, 1911), p. 3.

[26] *Reno Evening Gazette*, April 5, 1905, p. 2, c. 1 and July 22, 1911, p. 6, c. 6; *Fairview News*, January 12, 1907, p. 2, c. 2.

[27] *Reno Evening Gazette*, July 22, 1911, p. 6, c. 6; *Churchill County Standard* (Fallon), November 24, 1915, p. 1, c. 3.

[28] *Churchill County Standard*, August 9, 1916, p. 3, c. 6.

[29] *Reno Evening Gazette*, November 27, 1916, p. 8, cc. 1–2.

[30] See the *Metropolis Chronicle. Nevada State Journal* (Reno), January 30, 1955, Historical-Pictorial Supplement.

[31] *Record-Courier* (Gardnerville), July 10, 1908, p. 1, c. 1.

[32] John Koontz (comp.), *Political History of Nevada* (Carson City: State Printing Office, 1960), pp. 66–67.

[33] *Nevada State Journal*, September 15, 1912, p. 3, c. 7.

[34] Samuel P. Davis, *The History of Nevada* (Reno: The Elms Publishing Company, 1913), Vol. I, pp. 457–458.

[35] *Co-operative Colonist* (Fallon), July, 1916, p. 2.

[36] *Ballot Box* (Fallon), December 16, 1911, p. 1, c. 5.

[37] *Ballot Box*, September 9, 1911, p. 4, c. 4.

[38] *Ballot Box*, November 4, 1911, p. 1, c. 6.

[39] *Ballot Box*, May 18, 1912, p. 1, c. 1.

[40] *Ballot Box*, October 26, 1912, p. 1, c. 1.

[41] *Ballot Box*, November 23, 1912, p. 1, c. 1.

[42] *Progress Report 1944–1958: Fernley Soil Conservation District* (Fallon: Fallon Eagle-Standard, 1959), p. 3.

[43] Interview with S. R. Marean, Reno, Nevada, January 2, 1963.

[44] Interview with Samuel Platt, Reno, Nevada, December 11, 1962.

Chapter III

Promotion and Settlement
of Nevada City

MOST SUCCESSFUL cooperative settlements in the United States have resulted from great individual effort supplemented by the vitality of a particular religious faith. The organic bond between members was usually sealed by something more meaningful than the pragmatic expression of production and consumption. But the threads which moored even the most homogeneous peoples to a common life were always tenuous and uncertain. Therefore, to attempt to mold a number of strangers not previously educated or screened into a common family-community was quixotic. The people of Nevada City were like an audience brought together in a movie theater. All were anxious to experience a common stimulus, yet as individuals they were separate, detached, and anonymous. Nor was it only economic frustration and radical socialism which led so many to seek out the colony; rather, it was the arousing of human expectations—expectations which outstripped reality and thereby induced disappointment and even despair.

COLONY PROMOTION IN THE WEST

In the spring of 1916, Eggleston directed his first sales campaign toward the farmers of Churchill County. He never overlooked the necessity of gaining control of land and never underrated the influence of the local Socialist party. Local goodwill and general support for colonizing schemes worked to his advantage. On April 12, a front page article in the *Churchill County Standard* explained that the local success of A. Grant Miller, C. V. Eggleston, and L. V. Flowers in securing property "proved the wisdom of the selection of the district as a field for cooperative work." The article went on to say that not only were a hundred or more Llano colonists ready to move to Fallon, but Eggleston had acquired seventeen hundred acres of land from fifteen local property owners upon which to locate the new arrivals. Before the end of the year, the colony was to "count 1000 resident members, each being a head of a family of several."[1] In emphasizing the explosive growth of the colony idea, the *Churchill County Eagle* explained that 60,100 shares of capital stock had already been issued to local ranchers in exchange for their property.[2] Neither newspaper seemed disturbed by the frank admission on the part of the settlement leaders that one of the aims was to bring the Socialist party into dominance in Nevada.

The colony's recruiting agents assumed that socialists were instinctively joiners and that most could be sold stock in the Nevada venture. As promoters, optimists, and men of action, they believed that Nevada City could be peopled by door-to-door contact. Eggleston's chief assistant on the local scene was a close friend and colleague, W. I. DeLong. However, as the community expanded and livestock was acquired, DeLong became less of a saleman and more the overseer of the Churchill County property. Formerly secretary of the Eggleston-King Pigeon Company, DeLong had become a foreman in the livestock pavilion of the Pacific International Exposition at San Francisco in 1915. Later, he followed Eggleston to Los Angeles. When offered employment with the Nevada colony, he accepted and traveled to Reno in April, 1916. Soon thereafter he moved with his family to Fallon. Always a loyal supporter of Eggleston's policies, DeLong also gained the respect of his associates and particularly of colony farmers who recognized him as an experienced manager of livestock.

Another of Eggleston's longtime friends, L. V. Flowers, became the colony's chief sales manager in California. Flowers first settled in Sparks, and although a traveling promoter for the colony, he was active in building the local socialist organization. In early 1917, he moved with his family to Oakland and for a time directed the company's West Coast activities. Although Flowers remained Eggleston's closest friend and confidant, he disassociated himself from the colony during the summer of 1917 and a few months later moved to Seattle.

Soon after the colony was officially launched, Flowers and J. S. Harmon, former owner of the land upon which Nevada City was built, were assigned the sales territory of California. They worked the central valley from Fresno north, conducted meetings in the homes of well-known farmers, and provided news stories for local newspapers. Eggleston forwarded general directions and expense money from Fallon and followed up the personal contact with the appropriate literature. Occasionally, Flowers suggested that financial inducements be offered to certain community leaders, but the more dedicated socialists, he warned, "would without exception resent the idea of making a cent of commission on any business they might get for us."[3]

Eggleston believed in the profit motive. He argued that if commissions were promised as a matter of course to all local socialist officials, most would sell company stock, and the future of Nevada City would be assured. In early 1917, he printed five hundred contracts and declared: "I will proceed to appoint agents all over the United States without delay, but I want to put more in California than anywhere else." He urged Flowers to secure the services of one new agent a day. "If you establish a dozen a day you will not hurt anything."[4]

An elaborate and many sided program was designed to attract California socialists. Most significant were the various newspaper and journalistic accounts of the colony. In a series of articles entitled "Socialists Plan to Grab State," Flowers explained that the California commissioner of corporations had granted the Nevada group full privileges to sell stock in California because within a year the Nevada Colony Corporation had become the largest business institution in Nevada. He emphasized that socialists were being drawn to Fallon in numbers sufficient to insure the victory of the party ticket in 1918. The Flowers publicity program received valuable sales support from articles written by Charles Edward Russell, the famous muckraker of the meat industry and a close friend of Eggleston.

For California socialists who did not respond to newspaper publicity, to Flowers' community meetings, or to Eggleston's brochures, a letter was sent out from Fallon quoting Walter Thomas Mills. As a socialist author, world traveler, and president of the International School of Social Economy at Berkeley, Mills like many others had been feted by Eggleston and in return wrote favorably of the colony. "If I had not seen it all with my own eyes I would never have believed it possible . . . it is truly wonderful."[5]

If a California socialist took out a subscription to the Nevada City newspaper but did not buy stock in the colony, he was sent a special form letter. It explained that the foundation for a great "Socialist Republic" was being laid in the Lahonton Valley and further declared that the East and Midwest had already shown "unbounded enthusiasm" for the idea. Clearly the western socialists were overlooking a great opportunity "to enjoy socialism in our day." Even after a Californian bought stock in the colony and became an installment member at ten dollars per month, he was not allowed to rest but was forwarded yet another letter which explained that with the payment of his full membership fee he would be forever insured against unemployment, overwork, poverty, greed, and fear. Therefore, "why be selfish?" Why not become a company agent and extend happiness to friends and associates by selling Nevada colony stock?[6]

PROMOTIONAL CAMPAIGN IN THE MIDWEST

Despite the active sales work in California, Eggleston's promotional campaign was also directed toward the Midwest. The Nevada colony was to be national as well as regional in scope, and political as well as economic in perspective. During the spring of 1916, Eggleston traveled throughout the region and extended a personal invitation to the leading socialist publicists and writers to visit Nevada. He was partic-

ularly fortunate in gaining the enthusiastic support of Fred
D. Warren, the former editor of the *Appeal to Reason*.
With a weekly circulation that at one point exceeded
525,000, the *Appeal* was a Saturday night bible for socialists
throughout the United States and Canada. And with a sales
and production staff totaling a hundred persons, the paper
had become the largest single socialist employer of labor in
the United States.

The *Appeal* had led the protest movement of Midwest
socialists for two decades, and Fred Warren had been the
paper's most dynamic editor. The first number of the journal was published by Julius Wayland in Kansas City,
Missouri, in August, 1895, but the paper was soon moved to
Girard, Kansas. Wayland's earlier journal, the *Coming Nation*, had been the quasi-official organ for the Brotherhood
of the Co-operative Commonwealth. Wayland also had
founded the Ruskin colony in Tennessee and had unsuc-
cessfully attempted to persuade Midwest populists to accept the Brotherhood idea of locating colonies throughout
the West. His moralist, prohibitionist, earthy journalism
epitomized the social protest of the plains and catapulated
the *Appeal* into national prominence.[7] In 1904, Fred Warren
assumed the editorship, and in 1907, Eugene Debs joined the
staff thus further enhancing the journal's stature. In the
years before World War I, the paper led half a dozen major
campaigns for legal and social justice. Warren became a
Socialist hero in 1909 when he was sentenced to jail and
ordered to pay a $25,000 fine. Opposition to the court deci-
sion became so threatening that President William Howard
Taft exercised clemency by striking the sentence and reducing the fine to $100 (which Warren never paid). Warren
enjoyed Debs's support for the presidency in 1912, but the

eastern delegations questioned the choice, and to maintain party unity Debs was forced to accept the nomination.

After the election of 1912, Warren steadily lost interest in the *Appeal*. Founder Wayland was indicted on a morals charge and committed suicide, the government renewed the policy of harassment, and Debs resigned as feature writer and returned to Indiana. Finally, in 1914, Warren visited Europe and quite accurately assessed the hopeless position of the socialist organizations. By 1916, the drift toward war convinced him that American socialism would soon disintegrate; therefore, out of a feeling of desperation he was ready to embrace almost any program which offered even a slight hope of political survival. Furthermore, Warren had been favorably impressed with Nevada during his earlier speaking tours throughout the state. When offered stock in the colony plus a fee of two thousand dollars per year to edit the colony newspaper, he accepted and traveled to Nevada in July, 1916. Although Warren never became editor of the *Co-operative Colonist*, his articles during 1916 and 1917 gave the colony unquestioned socialist standing and a nationwide following.

Warren signed an explanatory letter asking for socialist support when Eggleston launched the *Co-operative Colonist* in March, 1916. He argued that European socialism had been "wiped out" by the war and that American socialism was about to experience the same fate. Therefore, the best alternative "I am almost persuaded to say: the only thing we can do, is to get together a little band of those who are willing to make sacrifices now, in a state like Nevada, that we may have peace and plenty later on for ourselves and our families." In Nevada the colony would raise its own food, build its own houses, and make its own clothes. Buying and selling "are the watchwords of capitalistic society" and the process which reduced the world to "savages and barbarians"; therefore, "we will buy as little as is absolutely necessary."[8] A few months later Warren wrote:

> The surest refuge for believers in peace will be the colony. It was so during the dark ages when Europe was deluged with blood and there was peace nowhere except in the religious colonies. It was the colony then that preserved what learning and art that has come to us from the storehouses of the past. It was not religion that did it so much as the refuge that the colony afforded. The colony may again become the harbor in which safe anchorage lies, the city of refuge to which the threatened may fly, the island in the midst of oceans of slaughter. Now is the time to prepare against war. Individually the best preparation is to seek the refuge of the colony.[9]

In late 1916, Warren returned to the escape theme. "Nevada appeals to me as a spot of refuge where the chances of working out our own Salvation are a shade better than in the states of New York, Illinois, Wisconsin or Kansas or any other state. For this reason I urge those of you who can to join with the pioneers in this work, and take this chance—this opportunity—while it is yet open."[10] Warren's comments grew even more poignant after war was declared. In his imagination, and it no doubt struck a responsive chord among those opposed to military service, Nevada provided a unique isolation from the arm of capitalistic militarism. In an article entitled "Mollie and the Babies," he explained: "Nevada alone seems immune, because of the barrier of the western mountains and the alkali desert on the south and the wide reaches of desert lands on the east. So those who don't want war to visit their fireside had better prepare a place for the wife and kiddies out in the mountains of Nevada."[11] Finally, in a full-page article of July, 1917, entitled "Your Last Chance," he pled: "Don't take my word for all this—come to Nevada and see for yourselves . . . it is the only thing left for us to do—our LAST CHANCE!"[12]

According to Warren, not only was the Nevada colony mankind's "last best hope" for survival, but equally as significant, Nevada was the New World's Switzerland. There were the same magnificent mountains, the same beautiful lakes, and the same sturdy people. In addition, "Nevada has wealth unsurpassed in its mountains" and "great, fertile valleys such as are not to be found in Switzerland." If the Swiss could maintain their integrity and democracy, said Warren, stay out of war and become self-sufficient, independent, and prosperous, so could Nevadans.[13] To assist in awakening the state to its true potential and great future, Warren and Eggleston decided to send the *Appeal to Reason* to every Nevada voter for one year. "Can you suggest a reason why all this cannot be done? Can you think of another state in the union, or of another country in the world, in which it could be done?" And in the great work of winning Nevada, "we are operating strictly in accordance with the principles of Marxian Socialism."[14]

Three of Fred Warren's assistants at Girard also became active supporters and publicists for the Nevada colony. Lincoln Phifer not only wrote widely for the colony, but in the tradition of the social reformer advocated correspondence schools, reading improvement courses, chautauquas, and psychoanalysis. He was for a time publisher of the *New World* also located at Girard. To Phifer, socialism was both a political method and a social faith. It was a party and a way of life. But Phifer advanced the revolutionary creed as well, and he delighted in spreading the rumor that Leon

Trotsky had secretly settled in Girard and was helping to direct socialism's cooperative programs.[15]

Eli N. Richardson was the first literary figure to join the colony. He had for several years assisted Warren in publishing the *Appeal*, but during the autumn of 1916, he moved with his wife and children to Fallon. Born on an Illinois farm in 1862, Richardson had been a baggage boy, a freight agent, and finally a station master and telegrapher on the Illinois Central Railroad. In 1884, he traveled west and after the turn of the century became a feature writer for the *New York Herald*, *St. Louis Globe Democrat*, *Kansas City Times*, and other publications. Being caught up in the populist and later the socialist agitation, Richardson was instinctively drawn to Fred Warren and the Girard enterprise. At Nevada City he first assisted Eggleston with the *Co-operative Colonist* and the *Nevada Colony News*, and under Bray's regime, he directed the colony's bond-selling campaign. With the collapse of the society, Richardson moved to Tonopah where he became business manager for the *Tonopah Daily Times Bonanza* and the southern Nevada correspondent for numerous metropolitan papers.[16]

Ben F. Wilson was the fourth member of the Girard phalanx to assist in the promotion of Nevada City. As a former preacher and onetime populist, Wilson became one of the leading socialist orators of his day, and as a member of the Kansas state legislature, he was respected for his able presentation of the socialist position. Wilson's Nevada speaking tours always drew large and enthusiastic crowds in Churchill County.

H. H. Stallard and the Oklahoma encampments were second only to Fred Warren and the *Appeal* in gaining midwestern support for the Nevada colony. As the backwash from the farmers' revolt rolled across the prairie states, the Socialist party attempted to capture and channel the discontent and provide social relief for farmers benumbed by isolation and worn out by drudgery. About 1908, a young socialist, Frank O'Hare, conceived the idea of annual encampments. The movement was instantly successful. People for miles around congregated at the encampment site, pitched tents, and proceeded to combine the revival meeting, square dance, basket dinner, and chautauqua into a force for political action. In 1916, the widely known Kansas socialist, H. H. Stallard, was appointed the Nevada colony's Oklahoma representative. A headquarters was established at Snyder, colony literature disseminated throughout the state, and a schedule of regional encampments circulated to socialist leaders. County officers were responsible for community advertising and local arrangements. Warren, Stallard, Ben Wilson, Lincoln Phifer, and others orated on politics, war, and radical doctrine, but they also emphasized the unique opportunity to put socialism into action through membership in the Nevada colony.[17]

The third major arm of the colony's midwestern publicity program was directed by Phil Wagner, managing editor of the *Social Revolution*. In 1912, Wagner, as manager of the *National Rip-Saw*, had asked Frank O'Hare, of Oklahoma encampment fame, to assist him on the St. Louis monthly. O'Hare employed his famous wife, Kate Richards O'Hare, as a co-worker. Harassed by the government because of an antiwar policy, the periodical in March, 1917, appeared as the *Social Revolution*, but in July it was again censored and Kate Richards O'Hare indicted because of further antiwar activities. To most of its 150,000 subscribers the journal represented one of America's leading crusaders for freedom of speech and press. Also during the spring of 1917, Phil Wagner accepted an invitation to visit Nevada, and later in the summer he became the colony's publicity director at a salary of $125 per month, plus two cents for every copy of his journal in which the colony was advertised. Although more circumspect than Warren, Wagner became convinced of the merits of cooperative colonies. Upon returning to St. Louis, he declared it his duty to inform *Social Revolution* readers that the Lahonton Valley was beautiful, properous, and healthy, and that the Fallon colony was a great success. In return for the favorable articles, Nevada colony members contributed handsomely to the O'Hare-Wagner campaign to provide legal counsel for all political prisoners in the United States including Kate Richards O'Hare.

In securing the support of Fred D. Warren with his *Appeal to Reason*, of Phil Wagner with his *Social Revolution*, and of H. H. Stallard and the Oklahoma encampments, Eggleston elevated the Nevada colony to a truly national status. By 1917, the midwestern publicity program had far outdistanced Flowers' sales campaign in California. The colony's most significant single advertising venture, however, had not proved completely successful.

PUBLICITY THROUGH THE "CO-OPERATIVE COLONIST"

Although in contact with a lengthy list of prospective colonists, Eggleston also gained access to the mailing list of Llano's *Western Comrade*, and on March 20, 1916, he launched the *Co-operative Colonist*. The journal was designed to become a major publicity organ for Nevada City, but it received a generally unenthusiastic reception. As an introductory offer, Eggleston sent five subscription cards at twenty cents per card to key individuals. A letter explaining the new journal and the Nevada colony accompanied the subscription blanks. The recipients, who were widely scattered throughout the United States, were asked either to sell the additional four cards or purchase all five for one dollar and give the extra subscriptions to friends. Of 584 socialists receiving a total of 3,000 subscription cards, approximately 6 percent actually sold the cards and returned the money. An additional 12 percent demonstrated interest in the project by returning the unsold cards. Throughout 1916, however, Eggleston continued to send out blank subscription forms for the colony's paper. Indeed, the system of payment was so loosely handled that anyone could sign the form and receive the *Colonist* free. One Oklahoma socialist made the collecting of subscription blanks to the *Colonist* into something of a hobby. Within a year he claimed to have amassed 400 cards.[18] But despite Eggleston's vigorous methods, the journal never enjoyed a truly large circulation.

On March 7, 1917, a year after the first publicity campaign, there were 478 paid subscribers in thirty-eight states, Alaska, and Canada. The *Colonist* was beginning to attract more support, however. Between February 20 and March 7, 1917, 178 new subscribers were added to the list. On the one day, February 21, twenty-nine orders for the paper were received.[19] Furthermore, none of the persons in the colony or in the Fallon area were included in the official ledger. The editor consistently reported that 3,500 copies of the paper were printed each month, and considering the large number of copies sent out as publicity, the statement was probably accurate. Indeed, during the autumn of 1916,

16,000 copies of the August issue were distributed throughout Nevada in an effort to elect A. Grant Miller to the United States Senate.

Many attempts were made to expand the *Colonist*'s circulation by capitalizing on the popularity of other socialist papers. In return for a subscription to *Pearson's Magazine* and the *Colonist*, the *Appeal to Reason* was offered free. Or if the subscriber already received the *Appeal*, it would be sent to a Nevada voter free. Or for a subscription of two years to the *Colonist*, the *Appeal* would be sent to a Nevada voter for one year free. Whatever the details, everyone was to receive the *Colonist* and be provided with a means for helping to carry Nevada for socialism.

During the spring of 1917, Eggleston experienced difficulty in getting the *Colonist* entered as second-class matter at the Fallon post office. Not only were all socialist papers carefully screened, but the *Colonist* had become almost totally an advertising medium for the colony. Therefore, in March, 1917, he founded another monthly, the *Nevada Colony News*, to meet the needs of the local colonists and to publicize their work. The *Colonist* was to become a socialist journal of national prominence. However, when Eggleston resigned as president of the board of directors, the *Nevada Colony News* was immediately discontinued.

PROMOTIONAL PROGRAM OF R. E. BRAY

Eggleston relinquished his personal control over Nevada City on June 12, 1917, and the new editor of the *Colonist*, R. E. Bray, quickly emerged as the dynamic force in most colony activities. Bray became particularly interested in the society's advertising program. Born in western New

York State in 1862, Bray homesteaded in Oklahoma in 1889 but within a few months deserted the land for Kansas politics. Working on the *Peoples' Voice* at Wellington and later on the *Hutcheson Gazette*, the young publicist led a delegation in the state convention which nominated "Sockless" Jerry Simpson for Congress. Later he returned to Oklahoma where he founded *Coming Events* at Enid and worked for numerous papers in Oklahoma City. After the turn of the century, Bray spent six years in the Florida pineapple business, assisted with the *Daily News* in Joliet, Illinois, the *Register* at Wayland, New York, and the *Constructive Socialist* at Alva, Oklahoma. He founded the *Southeast Missourian* at Hunter in 1913, but questionable promotional schemes and radical political doctrines led to local criticism and Bray's trip to Llano in 1915. At Llano he eagerly lent himself to the Eggleston designs and became one of the three founders of the second Nevada Colony Corporation. Returning, for a while, to Missouri to sell his paper, Bray arrived permanently in Nevada only a few weeks before Eggleston's resignation.

At first maintaining the friendship of Eggleston and representing the printing and advertising hope of the colony, the large, affable, and bewhiskered Bray became the directive force for the colony. Indeed, he became wedded to the society, and although he indulged in cheap theatrics and shady promotion, anyone who questioned the colony's purpose or progress became an enemy. In February, 1918, Bray moved from a comfortable Fallon home to an adobe house in Nevada City. Despite pneumonia, the extended illness of his wife, and the departure of his son for the marines, Bray as corresponding secretary continued to give personalized replies to ten or fifteen letters of inquiry a day. He helped to plant and tend the crops, stack alfalfa, compose and print the *Co-operative Colonist*, direct the financial and legal aspects of colony life, and, with the assistance of a colleague, milk some thirty-four head of colony cows. He relied upon personal persuasiveness and his Oklahoma friends to insure his continued control. Bray repeatedly stressed, "We want more Oklahoma comrades," and in January, 1918, he proposed that a campaign be launched to secure "500 from there [Oklahoma] by next May" because "they make the best boosters and colonists."[20]

Soon after Bray took over the direction of the *Colonist* he decided to place advertisements "in all of the Socialist papers of the country."[21] From the *Daily Call* of Seattle to the *Leader* of Fitchburg and Boston, Massachusetts, from the *Star* of Frackville, Pennsylvania, to the *Co-Operative News* of Everett, Washington, and from the *Sword of Truth* of Sentinel, Oklahoma, to the *Weekly Bulletin* of Butte, Montana, the story of Nevada's new order was told. In local papers like the *Argosy* of Belper, Kansas, in regional journals like the *Home and Farmer* of San Francisco, in specialized publications like the *Angora Journal* of Portland, Oregon, in the *Socialist Year Book of Cuyahoga County* of Cleveland, Ohio, and even in a woman's weekly printed only in Finnish, *Toveritor*, readers were informed that there was a community in Nevada that soon would have "greater power and influence than the Standard Oil Company."

Not all papers welcomed the colony business. For example, the *Co-operative Consumer* of New York City canceled the Nevada advertisement in May, 1918. They had previously given it a prominent display on the back of their journal, but the advisory council composed of John Dewey, Edward P. Cheyney, Walter Lippmann, and others checked the colony's references and financial statements and concluded that the project was unsound.[22]

The *Appeal to Reason* and the *Social Revolution*, along with the *Cooperative Herald* of St. Paul, stimulated the most widespread interest in the colony. Nevertheless, many local papers like the *York Labor News* (Pennsylvania) and the *Miami Valley Socialist* (Ohio) provoked a significant response. Although enjoying a circulation of only fifteen hundred, the *Co-Operative News*, formerly the *Northwest Worker* of Everett, Washington, contributed immensely to the Nevada experiment. Serving several strike-torn and embittered communities, the *Co-Operative News* kept a constant stream of letters flowing to Nevada City. *Svenska Socialism* of Chicago also directed considerable attention to the colony. Inquiries were received in both Swedish and German, and in many of the letters written in English, sentences were heavily interspersed with German words. On the other hand, neither *Tover*, the Finnish daily of Astoria, Oregon, nor the long articles in the *Colonist* devoted to the social progress in Finland aroused a response from Finnish-American communities.

In addition to his sweeping advertising program, Bray requested local and state Socialist committees to supply him with lists of prospective colonists. County officials were contacted in the Midwest, and the state secretary of the party in Texas was asked by a mutual friend to forward Bray a copy of his mailing list. Many of the local officers did not respond, and few were as cooperative as the chairman of the party in Cherokee County, Kansas, who supplied

at least three rosters of names. Bray, like Eggleston, requested installment members to conduct a selling campaign
among their friends. Although little company stock was
sold by the community agents, they were able to attract
dozens of new readers for the *Co-operative Colonist*. For
example, during the spring of 1918, W. L. Achberger of
Elkhart, Indiana, sold 20 subscriptions to the paper and received 100 shares of colony stock as a fee; Frank Gilliam of
Roseville, California, sold 50 subscriptions and received 250
shares of stock; and Albert Duke of Niter, Idaho, sold 200
subscriptions and received a prize of 500 shares of capital
stock.[23]

Under Bray's direction the colony printing plant became
a thoroughgoing advertising facility. In addition to the *Co-
operative Colonist*, the press produced thousands of leaflets,
brochures, and pamphlets and at the same time gained wide
notice through work done for outside organizations. When
H. A. Prinegar of Wellington, Utah, contracted to have
two thousand circulars printed to advertise his raspberry
plants, the colony supplied the mailing list in return for
which they received ten thousand plants and permission to
place a colony advertisement on the front page of the
brochure.[24]

The scattered printing records that have been preserved
point to a far-flung publicity program. On July 7, 1917, 500
copies of a four-page circular were produced; on July 23
the leaflet was re-ordered and 750 copies printed; and on
October 8 another 1,000 copies came from the press. Between July 23 and September 27, 1917, 1,800 copies of a
six-page circular were issued. Throughout the same period,
thousands of copies of a two-page circular, a circular letter,

a statement of assets, a brochure entitled "Facts About the Valley," a sheet on resources and liabilities, a leaflet entitled "Answers to Questions," and a forty-page booklet were liberally distributed throughout the country.[25]

Perhaps the most effective publicity program engaged in by Secretary Bray centered around his letter writing. Unlike Eggleston, Bray never used a form letter in his replies; rather, a highly individualized and personal touch became the hallmark of Bray's salesmanship. He had ample opportunity to practice his art. A total of 724 letters from 428 different prospective colonists have been preserved in the McCarran Papers. Scattered from January, 1917, through June, 1918, 85 percent of the correspondence falls in the nine months between October, 1917, and June, 1918, when Bray was colony secretary. With the discontinuance of stock sales on July 1, 1918, most inquiries ceased.

Clearly the letters now available are only a small fraction of the total number received; nevertheless, 428 queries from thirty-eight states, Alaska, Hawaii, and Canada provide a reasonably accurate picture of the type of person interested in the Nevada experiment. The letters also reveal the occupations of prospective colonists, the areas of the country where interest was most pronounced, and the reasons for joining the community.

The geographical correlation between subscribers to the *Co-operative Colonist* and letters of inquiry was quite high. Of the 478 subscribers to the *Colonist* on March 7, 1917, California led the list with 68, followed by Oklahoma with 42, Ohio with 30, Montana and Indiana with 28 each, and Washington and Illinois with 24 each. Of the 428 letter writers, there were 38 from California, 33 each from Oklahoma and Ohio, 31 from Washington, 24 from Pennsylvania, and 23 from Montana. In short, interest in the Nevada colony fell into three major geographical regions. Most significant from the standpoint of newspaper subscriptions and general correspondence was an arclike section of the American West extending from California north into Washington and then east to Montana. Most significant from the standpoint of migrants to Nevada City was an area centered in Oklahoma and including adjacent districts in Arkansas and Kansas. Most significant from the standpoint of industrial interest was an elongated region stretching from Chicago to Cleveland to Pittsburgh. The urban interest was supplemented by farm centers like Elkhart, Indiana; Findlay, Ohio; and York, Pennsylvania. Response in the New England states proved to be disappointing, and with the exception of Florida, no contact or publicity was attempted in the South Atlantic area.

The primary occupation of the prospective colonist was not always clear, but about 50 percent of the correspondents were involved in some phase of agriculture. Among those who wrote were dairymen, chicken fanciers, gardeners, prunepickers, and stockmen. Perhaps 10 percent were artisans; carpenters, bricklayers, and painters were in the majority. Another 10 percent were industrial workers; however, a large number of the factory personnel were carpenters, bricklayers, or mechanics by trade. About 20 percent of the inquiries were from insurance salesmen, printers, storekeepers, service personnel, and the retired. The professional and technical areas were represented with letters from authors, clergymen, an optometrist, a physician, a violin maker, and a piano tuner. Other inquiries were received from sailors, soldiers, capitalists, convicts, and atheists. The convicts and atheists failed to explain how their specialities would contribute to Nevada's communal society.

THE COLONY APPEAL

The peculiar blend of physical, social, and psychological needs which led so many to seek a cooperative life has often invited a subjective rather than an objective treatment. Nevertheless, there were at least six basic reasons for interest in the Nevada society. Economic conditions were paramount in the minds of a majority of the 428 correspondents. Socialistic beliefs excited a large number of letters, and many persons seemed to be interested in finding a healthful climate. A few of the eastern urban socialists expressed a wish to enjoy the true freedom supposedly found in a western agrarian society. Elderly people hoped to find a retirement home, and, as in all utopian programs, there were the professional joiners.

The economic motive was most often cited by farmers and artisans of the Great Plains and Far West. Unable to compete economically and facing continued adversity, scores of ranchers sought a haven in cooperation. Years of discouragement in trying to farm the dry plateau near Rudyard, Montana, left Adam Jackson only too anxious to follow Bray's *obiter dictum* of sell all and buy a ticket for Fallon.

> Dear Comrades, you may be surprised to hear that I have sold my property today and got one hundred down and I am to get the rest in twenty days. I have made a great sacrifice to sell it. . . . I will take your advice and not make an extra trip to look over the colony. Now comrade, I mean

that we will work out the balance of our shares. Would it be so that you could let us have a tent to live in until the colony has a house built for us? Please let us know if everything is satisfactory and then we will let you know when we will start from Rudyard.[26]

When J. H. Sanders of Laclede, Idaho, sent in five dollars as a first installment, he explained: "I am ready to try. Don't waste any postage on me for I am too anxious to join you now. Instruct me, but persuade me not to retreat from a monster [capitalism] that has defeated the world."[27]

But Fallon held out little encouragement for the extremely poor. A Texas letter reflected the despair of many would-be colonists.

> My dear Comrades, with a sincere feeling of brotherly love and comradeship I will write you once more. . . . It seems a hopeless case of my ever realizing the pleasure of living in your colony! I have tried to get work here, but hard times seem to forbid it. . . . I more than thank you, for the very kind and generous offers you have already made to me, but alas! I am not able, at least at present, to comply. I really can't see how I'm to make it, without help of some sort. I did not start writing this, with any expectation of getting a reply; more to thank you, as I said, for kindness already shown to me. But the "stream is not bridged" and I am somewhat in despair as to what I'll do.[28]

Belief in communal ideals was a second force which focused attention toward Fallon. Scores of loyal socialists saw the society as the realization of a dream. It was the buoyant philosophy of Nevada City which they found most attractive. A Canadian explained, "I have been tired of the cold world a long time. . . . I long for a bit of cooperation where I can be interested in others and them in me, a brotherhood indeed."[29] The owner-craftsman in a harness and glove shop in Oregon echoed similar sentiments when he wrote: "Comrade Bray and all the comrades, your letter makes me feel like life is worth living yet. It surely made my wife and self feel we had some friends that are willing to share life with others and try to make others happy. . . . We are coming with the intention of doing our best to make the colony a grand success."[30]

Brotherhood was also the key for many rural socialists. When F. M. Fletcher of Buffalo Hart, Illinois, learned that the colonists were making molasses, he longed to participate so that they could join together in eating "pork, corn-cakes and sorghum." It was a fare that would make his diet of "possum and sweet-taters pale into insignificance." Nevertheless, Fletcher was also a fighting socialist. When faced with community criticism for his political beliefs and his support of the Nevada experiment, he invested $1,420 in colony bonds and declared himself ready to be wrapped in the *Appeal to Reason*, using socialist books for a pillow and then "defy God Almighty, Hell, or the Devil to take issue" with him. "Nature is our God," and "in our old days we can look at Socialism, beaming with a thousand lights, and all will be proud of their efforts."[31]

A few of the Socialists saw in the colony an outlet for their ambitions. As a county chairman for the Socialist party in Kansas, George W. Snyder chafed at the necessity of working for a mutual insurance company. He longed for the day when he would become business manager at Nevada City: "For over twenty years I have devoted all of my energies to the problem of mastering co-operative business management. . . . I have also the legal experience of over ten years of legal practice, during which time I got to the bottom of the legal questions involved, and now I must waste those talents and experience in the narrow rut of a company that devotes its energies to the miserably little potatoes, of so-called MUTUAL INSURANCE. It simply is galling."[32]

More radical elements viewed the society as the beachhead from which the final onslaught against capitalism was to be launched. Their letters emphasized that they were among the "red card men of America." Occasionally the colony's "red agents" met with considerable opposition. One in Texas was "subjected to the everlasting Hellish persecution of the powers that be." After being detained in jail for several weeks, he apologized for having sold neither stock nor subscriptions to the *Colonist* but assured the colony that although "a little disfigured" he was "still in the ring."[33] After visiting the colony in 1916, a Wisconsin socialist made plans to join the society; however, when war was declared he concluded that there was insufficient time to build the society in Nevada. The world was collapsing and all must have "the courage and the brains to go ahead and take over the state while there is yet an opportunity."[34]

The colony often arranged to use socialist propagandists as indirect promoters for Nevada City. When W. R. Duncan of Lewiston, Montana, bought stock in September, 1917, he agreed personally to publicize the colony throughout Montana. As an organizer for the National Nonpartisan League, Duncan lectured to farm groups, and although the league was listed as nonpartisan, it uniformly supported Socialist candidates. Bray hoped to bring Duncan and Ben Wilson, who represented the league in Kansas, to Nevada City to use them and their organizations to gain socialist support for the colony. The St. Paul headquarters for the league deferred launching a campaign in Nevada, however, and as the war progressed the influence of the organization tended to decline.

Climate was a third major force in the building of the colony. Almost every issue of the *Co-operative Colonist* carried one or more articles stressing the healthful climate and pleasant weather of western Nevada. During the particularly mild winter of 1917–1918, Bray's weather charts and reports of farming activities excited much interest in the midwestern and eastern states where the winter was unusually severe. The suggestion that strawberries were growing as large as pumpkins and that February had become the best month for gardening were examples of Bray's humor. But the more than two dozen inquiries asking for information on the Fallon weather point up the magnetism which a sunny climate exerted on thousands of snowbound socialists.

The legendary independence of the West coupled with the freedom supposedly provided by socialism supplied a fourth inducement for joining the colony. Few advocates of cooperation remained as true to the Nevada ideal as the eastern industrial workers. As an employee in the armor plate division of Carnegie Steel Corporation at Homestead, Pennsylvania, George Rumbold applied for membership in the colony and in the Socialist party in November, 1916. He had delayed both actions until he became an American citizen. Rumbold and a friend, Thomas McGee, also of Homestead, continued their monthly installment payments to the colony until April, 1919. In 1917, Rumbold publicized the society at peace meetings and woman suffrage groups in the Pittsburgh area, and as an ardent Socialist and cooperator, he wrote to Eggleston in April, 1917: "You can't feed me too much news of the colony. . . . We reds are likely to be weeded out by the steel trust most any time; personally I know I only hold my job by my ability to produce. I just hope they won't disturb me, till I get enough to carry me and mine to Fallon."[35] Rumbold sold subscriptions to the *Colonist* and installment contracts; he enlisted his German-born sister and brother-in-law in the colony and bitterly resented being "forced by the steel trust to buy liberty bonds" instead of being allowed to purchase "freedom bonds" in Nevada City.

Convinced of the need for social revolution, the Pennsylvania socialists along with others in Ohio and Indiana accepted cooperation as the solution for their discomfiture and then worked desperately to sustain their beliefs and discipline themselves against the war prosperity which surrounded them. Such socialists created a vision which they could neither realize nor abandon. They greeted the colony's failures as minor annoyances, and when the *Colonist* ceased publication in September, 1918, they refused to believe that the experiment had failed, and argued that government authorities had denied the colony mailing privileges.

A fifth motive for colony settlement, and an important internal problem, centered around the large number of elderly people who viewed cooperation as a synonym for retirement. Somewhat paradoxically the older and supposedly more conservative element in society expressed greater enthusiasm for cooperation than the younger generation. However, young adults often saw the colony as a happy solution for the retirement of their parents. In several instances pensioners hoped to grant the colony their monthly income in exchange for retirement privileges. One gentleman from Ohio who received sixty dollars per month "from Standard Oil, as a reward for 27 years of slaving for the company," thought it only fitting that Standard Oil money should help build the socialist institution that was to destroy capitalism.[36] Others proposed making the colony the beneficiary of a life insurance policy or of making a will in favor of the society. A surprisingly large number of elderly men with relatively young wives and large families of small children made application for membership. Several unorthodox agreements were executed under Eggleston's management, but after June, 1917, a rather strict plan to refuse admittance to elderly applicants was followed.

A sixth group attracted by the Nevada experiment were the social reformers, the maladjusted, the angry, and the professional joiners. Inasmuch as Nevada City was to provide employment for the unemployed, hope for the distressed, and humanity for mankind, it drew the attention of a score of unique groups and individuals. The colony was founded at a time of great social, political, and economic upheaval at every level of national life. The unexcelled publicity program was designed to attract a divergent following, and even the remoteness of Nevada provided a timely appeal. Among the uncommitted, the perchless travelers, and the rural rebels, interest in collective doctrines was widespread. Of course, all social undertakings attracted the misfits, the do-gooders, the joiners, the has-beens, and the ne'er-do-wells. Communal settlements were the natural haven for the pacifists, the temperance advocates, the vegetarians, the religious fanatics, the educational faddists, and the medical experimenters. The faith often placed in the colony's ability to reconstitute society was amazing.

A surprisingly small percentage of the Nevada colonists

had been associated with other socialist or cooperative colonies. Letters were received from members of the Ruskin settlement in Tennessee and the Helicon Home Colony of New Jersey, but none of the eastern cooperators traveled to Fallon. Several persons at the Straight-Edge Industrial Commonwealth at Alpine, New Jersey, planned to move to the colony, but could not amass sufficient funds.[37] Numerous former Llano cooperators were represented, however. By placing T. Osborne Angell in charge of construction and making F. H. Gallup bookkeeper, Eggleston lured the first Llano colonists to Fallon in 1916, but he was generally unsuccessful in attracting others from the Los Angeles settlement until it began to collapse in 1917. In early March, 1917, seven members of the Harriman colony arrived in one day, and some twenty made application to exchange Llano stock for Nevada stock. Eggleston, apparently hoping to gain control of the California colony, allowed the trade. During the summer and autumn of 1917, a few prospective Llano settlers turned to Fallon after learning, upon their arrival in California, that the Llano society was planning its trek to Louisiana. Despite the many who arrived, only some three or four of the Llano group remained in Nevada City more than a few weeks.[38] However, of the 428 persons requesting information from the Nevada colony, at least 17 of the writers had visited Llano and in disappointment were turning to Fallon. Conversely, at least two residents of Nevada City deserted to join the Newllano experiment in Louisiana.

The Nevada colony did not limit its appeal to areas of contemporary discontent but also sought support from older communal societies in the East. The colony at Ephrata, Pennsylvania, was founded by the Dunkard, Conrad Beisel, in 1728. Over the following years it grew into an important socio-religious organization, but by 1917 the oldest cooperative in the United States was reduced to about twelve members. Although the colony had virtually disappeared, the philosophy lingered on, and persons of the area became attracted by the German influence and antiwar policy at Nevada City. R. O. Fahnestock of Ephrata became a stockholder in the Fallon community and distributed the *Co-operative Colonist* among his Pennsylvania brethren. He assured Eggleston: "I will endeavour to instill into them the new vision. . . . I will do all I can to develop the vision in Lancaster County." After war was declared, Fahnestock conceded the prophetic wisdom of Fred Warren's articles and agreed that colony life provided the only hope of avoiding American militarism.[39]

Organized religion often created a dilemma for colony leaders. The pragmatic approach was followed, however, and no position ever taken. One of the society's most helpful advertising media in the Northwest was the *Crucible* of Seattle. The paper demanded that laws requiring Sunday observance be repealed, that the reading of the Bible in public schools be prohibited, that church property be taxed, that government employment of chaplains cease, and that court oaths be discontinued. The *Crucible* negated Christ, divine revelation, and the supernatural.[40] It emphasized that socialism was rationalism and natural law. The *Crucible* attracted socialists who sought the dawn of a new age of reason. And yet in the same period, Nevada City appealed to equally extreme social-Christian rebels like J. D. Newton. As a preacher-farmer in Arkansas, Newton failed because, he said, the "nigger-loving Democrats" drove him out. Although without funds, he nevertheless argued that if truly socialist the colony would accept him and his large family because the "Great Socialist" had said, "Whosoever will may come." If denied admission at Fallon, he would remain a man in "capitalistic bondage" destined to be a slave until a new order would "share the wealth."[41]

Both Mormon and Catholic correspondents expressed concern over the apparent lack of religious life in the colony. Generally, however, one or two members of the particular faith could be produced who would emphatically deny any antireligious sentiment. One Seventh Day Adventist withdrew from the society when she found the Lahonton Valley without a church of her denomination. Vegetarians were equally disturbed over the meat-eating propensities of the colonists, and although several from California's Imperial Valley became installment members, none settled permanently at Fallon.

Advocates of "one world" were fascinated by Fallon when they learned that Esperanto classes were to make the colony truly international in character. Fred Rivers, formerly of the Symbol Publishing Company, Esperanto printers of Tacoma, Washington, became so enamored with the idea that he offered to become the instructor and exchange his typewriter and other personal effects for company stock. But Bray's demand for five hundred dollars in cash dampened Rivers' enthusiasm and brought an end to the Esperanto program.[42] Blind persons were equally disappointed when the widely publicized school for the blind failed to become a reality.

At least one member of the Anti-Cigarette League of America (headed by Thomas A. Edison, Judge Ben Linsey, and David Starr Jordan) joined the colony as an installment member. As business manager for the *Seattle Daily Call*, T.

C. Mauritzen placed advertising in several papers of the Northwest and attempted to recruit antitobacco colonists for Nevada City. Many critics of tobacco were sorely disappointed to find that both Dr. A. C. Adams and Dr. F. B. Harrison of the colony were heavy smokers. But they were delighted when the society's directors declared that tobacco could not be used at colony board meetings.

Even men in the armed services became interested in a plan which insured their future. By merely paying installments while in service they were guaranteed a home and employment for the remainder of their lives. Several soldiers expressed interest, but only one actually became an installment member. A Texas socialist who had joined the navy suggested that he be given a colony membership in return for land which he would homestead and give to the community after the war. In the meantime he agreed to circulate the *Co-operative Colonist* among the men at the Great Lakes Training Station and direct their thoughts toward communal settlement in Nevada. "This war is making radicals out of nearly every man in the service, but as yet there is no purpose to their unrest, just a blind protest."[43]

J. B. Douglas, a prisoner at Leavenworth, Kansas, expressed a similar wish to direct his associates toward cooperation. As a socialist from Calvin, Oklahoma, he was one of a group sent to the penitentiary for refusing to be conscripted. After studying the colony literature, several at Leavenworth indicated they were anxious to join the experiment. Douglas suggested that Bray explain the organization to a sister in Oklahoma so that upon his release all could meet at Nevada City. In reply Bray counseled, "Be of good cheer and when you have earned your freedom, we hope to have here a refuge where you can come and help us to build an institution which shall be a beacon to the rest of the toilers throughout the land."[44]

The first colonists to be attracted to the Lahonton Valley began to arrive in late May, 1916. At the first annual meeting of shareholders, held on November 14, forty-seven members were present; most were from the Fallon area. There were five Baumanns, four Harmons, and three Egglestons represented as stockholders. Actually, only eight or nine families from outside the valley had settled at the colony. Relatively few new members came in during the winter and spring of 1917, but some two dozen families arrived during the summer and early autumn. By October 1, 1917, there were forty-four comrades with accounts at the commissary, and only three or four were former residents of the town of Fallon. Eight families entered the colony between October 1 and December 31, 1917, and nine left. During January, 1918, five families arrived at Nevada City, and the community reached its maximum size of some forty-eight stockholders or approximately two hundred persons.[45] The population declined rapidly during March and April but tended to level off at about twenty-five families throughout the summer and early autumn. In October and November, 1918, there was a further exodus with about half of the colony leaving. But despite the mounting dissatisfaction, new members continued to arrive. Nineteen families settled at the colony between February 1 and December 31, 1918. The last arrival was on February 17, 1919. In April, 1919, the commissary was still open, and eleven colonists were working and recording their hours of labor on the monthly time report forms.[46] Although the colony went into receivership on May 1, 1919, several persons remained at Nevada City through the summer of 1919, and two or three families lived in "adobe village" until early 1920.

In an attempt to set forth clearly the company assets and liabilities, a list of colony members was compiled in May, 1919. It indicated that in the three years, May 1, 1916, to May 1, 1919, ninety-five stockholders had settled at the colony. Most local participants like the Harmons, the Baumanns, the Egglestons, W. I. DeLong, L. V. Flowers, and A. Grant Miller were not included on the list, and several other colonists who had lived at Nevada City were overlooked. If all had been catalogued, the roster of stockholders would have totaled approximately 125 names. Families varied in size from one to thirteen persons, but averaged about four and one-half persons per registered stockholder. Therefore, there was a total of some 562 individuals who resided in the colony sometime between May 1, 1916, and May 1, 1919.

No running account of the number of members who contributed to the project through installment contracts remains; however, at the time of foreclosure, a "current" list of 145 persons from thirty-three states and Canada was prepared. Nineteen of the installment members were from California, fourteen from Montana, twelve each from Washington and Pennsylvania, and ten from Oklahoma. Funds continued to be received throughout 1918 and until April, 1919. Twenty-four persons made payments as late as June, 1918, nineteen in September, eight in November, and five in March, 1919.[47] Although records on installment purchases were inadequately kept, a list of proxies sent in before the stockholders' meetings of November, 1917, and November,

1918, reveal that only about one-third of the names on the proxy lists were included on the "current" list of May, 1919. Furthermore, dozens of letters which accompanied installment payments have been preserved, and the names of a large number of the contributors do not appear on the May list. It would seem, therefore, that there were about three times as many installment members as recorded on the May, 1919, list; or approximately 435 expectant colonists bought stock on the installment plan. Since each stockholder represented an average of four and one-half persons, nearly 2,000 people became members of the colony in absentia.[48]

The first members of the Nevada Colony Corporation were Fallon ranchers and California organizers who together founded the settlement. During the summer of 1916, several persons from the Sparks area and a few Californians moved to the community. By late 1916 and early 1917, the new members were coming from widely scattered regions of the West and Midwest, but later in 1917, the Oklahoma contingent began to overshadow all other elements. When Nevada City reached its maximum population in January, 1918, fifty-eight of the approximately two hundred residents were natives of Oklahoma. Indeed, forty-five years later, when speaking of the community, several persons who had observed the experiment from neighboring ranches referred to it as "the Okie colony."

Other Fallon ranchers remember the settlement as "the German group." Many of the early articles and several of the socialist ideas reflected in the *Co-operative Colonist* were German-oriented. Gustav Schulz, a former German-born resident of Montana, argued that the overthrow of capitalism was at hand and that the colony was the instrument by which it should be accomplished. Another Ger-

TABLE 1

NONRESIDENT INTEREST AND PARTICIPATION IN COLONY

State	No. of letters of inquiry preserved in McCarran Papers[a]	No. of individuals who wrote letters listed in first column[a]	No. of subscribers to the *Colonist* March 7, 1917 (Fallon excluded)	No. of active installment members on Sept. 30, 1917	No. of installment members carried by colony May, 1919[b]
Ala.			5		
Alaska	1	1	6	1	2
Ariz.	5	5	6	2	2
Ark.	16	6	6	6	7
Cal.	67	38	68	10	19
Canada	5	5	7	2	2
Colo.	20	15	14	1	2
Conn.	1	1			
Cuba			12		1
Fla.	13	7	1	1	1
Ga.					1
Hawaii	1	1			
Idaho	37	17	15	4	3
Ill.	31	14	24	3	5
Ind.	24	13	28	1	2
Iowa	8	6	8	2	2
Kan.	28	15	21	2	5
Ky.	5	4	1		1
La.	5	5	4		
Maine			1		
Mass.	5	4	1	1	1
Mich.	18	14	13		2
Minn.	11	9	12	2	3
Miss.	3	2	4		1

State					
Mo.	9	7	6	1	2
Mont	36	23	28	10	14
Nebr.	7	5	2	2	3
Nev.	14	10	6	5	6
N.H.	.	.	3	.	.
N.J.	5	4	4	.	2
N.M.	3	3	2	.	1
N.D.	14	6	6	.	1
N.Y.	14	8	11	1	1
Ohio	54	33	30	4	6
Okla.	52	33	42	10	10
Ore.	38	20	14	1	4
Penn.	54	24	15	10	12
R.I.	1	1	.	.	.
S.D.	5	5	6	.	1
Tenn.	2	2	.	.	.
Tex.	18	12	15	3	4
Utah	29	10	6	2	3
Wash.	54	31	24	8	12
W. Va.	5	4	1	.	.
Wis.	4	3	2	.	.
Wyo.	2	2	4	2	2
Unknown	.	.	.	7	.
Total	724	428	478	104	145

a Represents an estimated one-third of the total number of inquiries made.
b Represents approximately one-third of the total number of installment members.

man, Albert F. Meissner, explained the colony's happy merging of utopian socialism into Marxian socialism. By late 1917, German-Americans like Gustav Boehm, Jr. and William T. Held of Philadelphia, John Kormier and Grant Deitz of Missouri, along with Peter Schneider of Hungary, Fred Venth of Germany, and the Baumanns of Switzerland, formed a significant German-speaking element. Peter Hiibel, Adam Frederick, C. T. Kline, George Weigel, Mat Schroder, Louis Rosenblith, John Vledder, R. J. Kolstrup, and J. J. Weigmann, while not all at the colony at the same time, nevertheless helped to provide a distinctive German flavor. Considerable correspondence was conducted in German, and at least one person at the colony spoke only German. The German community in Douglas County, although vigorously antisocialist, carefully followed the society's program. There were more letters of inquiry from Minden and Gardnerville than from all other Nevada communities combined.

Obviously, both the international socialist tradition and the antiwar doctrines of the colony were found attractive by many German groups. In the prewar period, colony leaders made a special effort to appeal to the German element. Eggleston emphasized that the community was to be physically arranged on the German plan and that its basic tenets were American adaptations of European doctrines. Despite the war hysteria and Bray's motto of "Beat the Dutch," there were no anti-German incidents involving the colony and only one or two petty squabbles involving colony children at the Harmon elementary school.

Although few Swedes arrived at Nevada City, many throughout the United States expressed interest in the colony's radical views. As natives of Sweden, the C. E. Andersons of Clipper, Washington, were familiar with floods, cold, snow, and dark forests, but they could not compete with authorities who harassed their friends and threw their socialist leaders into jail. Nevertheless, Mrs. Anderson assured Bray, "I have read the literature you sent me, over and over, many times, and have every point in my memory, and can relate it to others that I happen to find interested."[49] The advertisements in *Svenska Socialism* spurred Swedes to make inquiry, but most were financially unable to pursue the idea. Frederic Comstock, a proofreader for *Collier's Weekly*, explained that he had read everything dealing with politics written in Swedish, German, or English and had been "a red socialist for 24 years." However, his European experiences led him to believe that the government would destroy the community. If it did not, he would leave for Nevada within a few months.[50]

Only one Frenchman traveled to Fallon, and, with characteristic charm, he likened the valley to a beautiful oasis in the French Sahara.[51] James Whitebread, an English machinist who had lived in Saskatchewan for fourteen years, joined the colony in August, 1917. With a son in the British army and his wife in England, Whitebread remained only a few weeks but declared that he would return with the family after the war. Many Canadians corresponded with colony officials, but only Edward Brock of Saskatchewan and John Campbell of Alberta moved to Nevada. Brock enjoyed the distinction of being the only colonist to have borrowed money from the company. Not only was the two hundred dollars never repaid, but as manager of the Humboldt ranch, he purchased building materials, tools, food, and other supplies at Lovelock without authorization and charged them to the society. When Robert Schafer, a longtime prospector from Valdez, Alaska, and Paul Ivanuck, an active socialist from the Isle of Pines, Cuba, arrived at Nevada City, the American continent had been joined. Publicists contended that Fallon had become a kind of geographical center as well as the ideological heart of North America. But the new order was not to extend to Asia. The request of O. J. Jang to learn about "communism and socialism" at Fallon so that he could "establish a colony in China" was denied.[52]

SIX WHO JOINED THE COLONY

The basic life and character of the Nevada colony can be easily distorted by overemphasizing the queer, the quaint, or the curious. In the final analysis it was not Germans, Oklahomans, atheists, or antitobacconists who fashioned the community. Perhaps the colony's attractions and its weaknesses can best be understood by studying a few of the families who settled at Nevada City.

Emigrating from England in the 1760's, the progenitor of Robert Ellis secured a land grant and settled in the North Carolina uplands. A century later the family had moved to Tennessee where Daniel Ellis was known as a participant in the underground railroad. Robert Ellis grew up as a coal miner in East Tennessee but moved to Ohio in the 1880's where he alternated between mining and farming. In 1898, Ellis left his family to seek work at Cripple Creek, Colorado. He returned to Ohio in 1899, but seventeen years later, when he read of the Llano settlement, he again started west. While traveling to California, a fellow passenger told him of the new colony at Fallon. Ellis stopped in western Nevada and was delighted with the Lahonton Valley. Marietta

Ellis and the children arrived in January, 1917, and three months later on April 20, Lois Ellis became the first child to be born at Nevada City. On June 13, the colony directors selected Ellis as a replacement for Eggleston on the board of directors and later the same day elevated the new director to the presidency of the colony. Although a mild critic of the aggressive policies of both Eggleston and Bray, Ellis drew great satisfaction from the cooperative effort and was delighted at being able to put his socialism into practice. As a member of no faction and disinterested in politics, Ellis was defeated for reelection to the board at the stockholders meeting of November, 1917. He remained an ardent supporter of the colony, however. With the rapid collapse of the society in September, 1918, he packed his wife and seven small children into a Ford car and left for the mines of northern Michigan. Although Marietta Ellis had disapproved of the colony idea and had at first abhorred life in Nevada, the family eagerly returned to Fallon in 1921.[53]

Peter Schneider was born in Hungary in the 1880's. He was the youngest of six children; his mother died when he was three; and his father married a widow who also had six children. Receiving little attention from the stepmother, he grew to resent her unfairness and pious religiosity. He left home when twelve years old, worked at odd jobs in Budapest, and in 1906 migrated to St. Paul, Minnesota, and opened a grocery store. Not completely satisfied with either the economic or political outlook, he returned to Budapest. While visiting at the home of a sister, he met Anna Kopf; they were married, and with his young bride Schneider again sailed for St. Paul. In 1911, the family moved west and attempted farming near American Falls, Idaho. Drought, depression, and a belief in socialism rendered

Schneider defenseless against colony literature. They sold most of their property at public auction, accepted notes from the purchasers, and arrived at the colony on October 22, 1917. Since Schneider had once worked as a machinist, he was made the colony blacksmith, and the family was temporarily housed in the smithy. (The shop, now a cow shed, and the old cement-block Harmon ranch house are the only Nevada City buildings still standing.) Although the Schneiders moved into a new frame dwelling at Christmastime, the colony had failed to measure up to the standards set by a European socialist. In early March, 1918, one of the family's four children, six-year-old Anna, died and was buried in the colony cemetery on the Taylor ranch. Grief-stricken and destitute, Schneider decided to leave, but when his plan became known, the commissary discontinued his food supply. With pitchfork in hand Schneider demanded and was promptly issued rations, and by way of balancing the accounts the colony treasurer handed Mrs. Schneider a crocheted bag containing fifty cents as they left Nevada City on April 28, 1918. For two weeks the family occupied a Fallon house vacated by John Kormier, then moved on to Sparks where in less than two years Peter Schneider died.[54]

Although born near St. Louis, Missouri, John Henry Kormier did not learn English until he entered elementary school. As a young man he drifted to Oklahoma, became a part-time coal miner, and married Ida Miller of Kansas. After twenty years of mining and farming, Kormier determined to migrate to Oregon where, according to the brochures, a sea of grass stretched along the Columbia River. In 1914, the family loaded farm machinery and livestock into cattle cars and started for The Dalles. Through a misunderstanding the cars were sidetracked at Doyle, Plumas County, California. Tired of the long journey, Kormier drove his stock north and eventually settled along Davis Creek. Lured by the Nevada City advertisements in the *Appeal to Reason* and dissatisfied with California, Kormier visited the colony in August, 1917. He promptly returned to Davis Creek, sold his property, and in October arrived back at the settlement with his wife and seven children. Kormier enjoyed his work as a carpenter, and after a lifetime of isolation on Oklahoma and California ranches, the children were delighted with their many new friends. In early 1918, Kormier became extremely ill with typhoid fever, and while he was recuperating on March 6, his ninth child was born. In mid-April the family moved to Fallon and then on to Sparks where Kormier worked as a carpenter for the Southern Pacific Railroad until his death in 1932. As a devout Lutheran and Oklahoma populist, Kormier, like Schneider, maintained an interest in the German language and socialist principles throughout his life.[55]

The Illinois miner William Riggle, while employed near Moulton, Iowa, met and married Louvina Bell. Dissatisfied with local opportunities and in search of a new life, the young family left for Colorado in 1895. In 1907, they moved on to Reno where Riggle worked as a ranch hand and carpenter on the Southern Pacific Railroad. After a bitter strike, Riggle was unable to find steady employment, and in early 1916 he became attracted by the Fallon enterprise. Both William Riggle and his son Artie bought colony stock, and in July, 1916, the family moved to the large two-story house on the "Lower Ranch." Before leaving Sparks, Artie was voted a resolution of appreciation for his years of loyal service by the local Socialist party, and he agreed to remain chairman of the publications committee for the *Nevada Socialist*. Professing no religious faith, but active in community affairs, the Riggles envisioned the fertile land, the hard work, and the warm friendships of the colony as a happy contrast to the unequal battle with the railroad. Only after settling on the ranch did they learn of the Union Security Company, the commissions paid to promoters, and the misleading advertising. A few days before Christmas, 1916, the Riggles moved to Fallon and for several months secured employment on a government experimental farm. In the spring of 1917, they repurchased their home in Sparks, and the elder Riggle again sought work with the railroad. After serving a year in the army, Artie, in 1919, married Sophia Baumann, a young lady he had known while a cooperator at Fallon.[56]

Adolph Baumann was born in 1854 near Berne, Switzerland. As a youth he excelled as a marksman, but rather than instruct soldiers for the army, he followed the example of two brothers and emigrated to Canada. He married Martha Egger, also of Switzerland, and after the birth of three children decided to seek the more temperate climate of California. Later, the family moved from the Sacramento Valley to southern Oregon but eventually settled on a farm near Napa, California. While attending business college in Napa, Sophia Baumann lived with the Henry C. Taylor family, and when in 1907 the Taylors decided to homestead in the rapidly developing Lahonton Valley, the Baumanns soon followed. By the time of their arrival in Nevada, several of the eight Baumann children were old enough to homestead on lands adjacent to those of their parents. Both of the elder Baumanns had been reared in devout Lutheran families, and Mrs. Baumann remained strongly religious throughout her life. Fluent in three languages, widely read, and conscientiously opposed to war and the military establishment, Adolph Baumann had become a Christian Socialist. He practiced his philosophy and naively accepted the statements of less scrupulous men. After mortgaging his land to Eggleston, he also assisted five of his children to become stockholders in the corporation. As Eggleston's secretary, Sophia wrote attractive articles on the valley for the *Co-operative Colonist,* and Alex gained what was considered the exciting assignment of colony truck driver. The Baumann livestock and foodstuffs contributed significantly to the colony's apparent prosperity. By late 1916, the Baumanns had become one of Eggleston's, and later the colony's, most active antagonists. Sophia assisted in circulating pamphlets condemning the company and later baffled Bray by her anonymous letters of warning written to prospective colonists. The Baumanns remained close friends of most of the colonists, however. Mrs. Baumann's paper wreath provided the only flowers at Anna Schneider's funeral, and it was her block of marble out of which Peter Schneider made his daughter's gravestone. The Baumanns were the only ranchers who reclaimed all of their land and remained permanent residents of the valley.[57]

After the Franco-Prussian War, Peter Hiibel of Baden decided that immigration was preferable to living under a Prussian emperor. He eventually settled in Kansas, and his son, also named Peter, became a western cowboy who spoke German, consulted socialist literature, and carefully read the *Appeal to Reason.* Although Hiibel was reasonably prosperous, the *Appeal* quickly convinced him that the colony could furnish comradeship, culture, and security for his rapidly growing family. In October, 1917, he loaded thirty-three cattle into a stock car at Pebokee, Kansas, and started for Fallon. Despite a multitude of problems, some three weeks later Hiibel unloaded the cattle at Ocala and drove them the three miles to the colony's Humboldt ranch. Hiibel was pleased with Nevada City and returned to Kansas for the family, but complications delayed their moving to Nevada until May, 1918. A daughter was born soon after their arrival, and the breakup of the colony created many hardships. On May 10, 1919, Peter Hiibel received two calves valued at fifty dollars and some harness, and his venture with the Nevada Colony Corporation was ended. The family continued to live at "adobe town" for another year, however, while Hiibel sought work as a farmhand. He died at Fallon in 1928.[58]

In retrospect, society can express understanding for those humble and faithful cooperators who were guided by a sense of need and conviction to seek the promise of a utopian commonwealth in western America. As agrarian reformers, they did not put their faith in a God that failed, instead they engaged in a rearguard action against history. As humanitarians they hoped to embark upon the regeneration of society, but in a restricted setting. As internationalists they planned to illustrate a facet of life which would touch universal chords. And as isolated socialists, they longed for the brotherhood of true cooperation. But neither rectitude nor sincerity were of themselves sufficient to assure the success of an experiment impeded by industrialization, war, and national antagonism, and hampered by selfish organizers, inept administrators, and untrained cooperators.

NOTES

[1] *Churchill County Standard* (Fallon), April 12, 1916, p. 1, c. 4.

[2] *Churchill County Eagle* (Fallon), April 15, 1916, p. 1, c. 4.

[3] L. V. Flowers to C. V. Eggleston, March 8, 1917, in Miscellaneous No. 9 of the McCarran Papers in the Nevada Historical Society, Reno.

[4] C. V. Eggleston to L. V. Flowers, March 6, 1917, in Miscellaneous No. 9 of the McCarran Papers.

[5] Follow-up letter No. 1 in Propaganda Notebook of the McCarran Papers.

[6] Form G and Form H in Propaganda Notebook of the McCarran Papers.

[7] Howard H. Quint, *The Forging of American Socialism* (New York: Bobbs-Merrill Company, Inc., 1964), pp. 181–187, 190–195.

[8] Form letter from Fred D. Warren in Propaganda Notebook of the McCarran Papers.

[9] *Co-operative Colonist* (Fallon), August, 1916, p. 11.

[10] *Co-operative Colonist*, November–December, 1916, p. 2.

[11] *Nevada Colony News* (Fallon), April 1917, p. 3.

[12] *Co-operative Colonist*, July 1917, p. 4.

[13] *Co-operative Colonist*, August, 1916, p. 4.

[14] *Co-operative Colonist*, August, 1916, p. 9.

[15] Interview with S. M. Watts, Pittsburg, Kansas, March 23, 1964.

[16] James G. Scrugham (ed.), *Nevada: A Narrative of the Conquest of a Frontier Land* (Chicago: The American Historical Society, Inc., 1935), III, 130–131.

[17] Oklahoma form letter in Propaganda Notebook of the McCarran Papers.

[18] R. E. Bray to G. H. Gresham, December 8, 1917, in Subscription Card Record and Miscellaneous No. 7 of the McCarran Papers.

[19] Ledger No. 1951 in the McCarran Papers.

[20] R. E. Bray to W. W. Hornbeck, January 5, 1918, in Miscellaneous No. 2 of the McCarran Papers.

[21] R. E. Bray to Emeti Parras, January 22, 1918, in Miscellaneous No. 6 of the McCarran Papers.

[22] C. R. Cheyney to R. E. Bray, May 8, 1918, in Miscellaneous No. 6 of the McCarran Papers.

[23] *Co-operative Colonist*, April, 1918, p. 5.

[24] See correspondence between H. A. Prinegar and R. E. Bray extending through the autumn and winter of 1917–1918, in Miscellaneous No. 6 of the McCarran Papers.

[25] File Box in the McCarran Papers.

[26] Adam Jackson to Nevada Colony, August 20, 1917, in Miscellaneous No. 2 of the McCarran Papers.

[27] J. H. Sanders to Nevada Colony, March 29, 1918, in Miscellaneous No. 5 of the McCarran Papers.

[28] U. P. Huffman to Nevada Colony, September 9, 1917, in Miscellaneous No. 2 of the McCarran Papers.

[29] E. J. Chaband to Nevada Colony, June 2, 1918, in Miscellaneous No. 7 of the McCarran Papers.

[30] C. B. Grable to R. E. Bray, January 13, 1918, in Miscellaneous No. 7 of the McCarran Papers.

[31] F. M. Fletcher to R. E. Bray, October 29, November 3 and 12, 1917, in Miscellaneous No. 9 of the McCarran Papers.

[32] George W. Snyder to R. E. Bray, February 8, 1918, in Miscellaneous No. 5 of the McCarran Papers.

[33] I. N. French to Nevada Colony, September 10, 1917, in Miscellaneous No. 9 of the McCarran Papers.

[34] Letter from Madison, Wisconsin, March 2, 1917, in Miscellaneous No. 8 of the McCarran Papers.

[35] George Rumbold to Nevada Colony, April 16, 1917, in Miscellaneous No. 1 of the McCarran Papers. Some ten of Rumbold's letters to the colony have been preserved.

[36] Ray B. Hugus to Nevada Colony, November 30, 1917, in Miscellaneous No. 2 of the McCarran Papers.

[37] Theodore Atwood to Nevada Colony, May 18, 1918, in Miscellaneous No. 1 of the McCarran Papers.

[38] *Co-operative Colonist*, November, 1917, p. 2; C. V. Eggleston to C. W. McDade, March 12, 1917 in Miscellaneous No. 8 of the McCarran Papers.

[39] R. O. Fahnestock to Nevada Colony, April 9, 1917, in Miscellaneous No. 9 of the McCarran Papers.

[40] Charles D. Raymer to R. E. Bray, February 13, 1918, in Miscellaneous No. 7 of the McCarran Papers.

[41] J. D. Newton to R. E. Bray, September 26, 1917, in Miscellaneous No. 8 of the McCarran Papers.

[42] Fred Rivers to R. E. Bray, November 12, 1917, in Miscellaneous No. 1 of the McCarran Papers.

[43] E. M. Gleason, Jr., to Nevada Colony, October 11, 1917, in Miscellaneous No. 6 of the McCarran Papers.

[44] R. E. Bray to J. B. Douglas, December 7, 1917, in Miscellaneous No. 9 of the McCarran Papers.

[45] Day Book No. 3 and Ledger A in the McCarran Papers.

[46] Cash Record Book and Colony Agreements in the McCarran Papers.

[47] Cash Record Book in the McCarran Papers.

[48] Colony Agreements and Miscellaneous No. 7 in the McCarran Papers.

[49] Mrs. C. E. Anderson to R. E. Bray, April 30, 1918, in Miscellaneous No. 1 of the McCarran Papers.

[50] Frederick L. Comstock to Nevada Colony, April 19 and May 26, 1918, in Miscellaneous No. 7 of the McCarran Papers.

[51] *Co-operative Colonist*, October 1917, p. 1.

[52] C. W. Jang to Nevada Colony, November 5, 1917, in Miscellaneous No. 2 of the McCarran Papers.

[53] Interview with Leland Ellis, Fallon, Nevada, January 5, 1963; *Co-operative Colonist*, May, 1917, p. 7.

[54] Interview with Henry Schneider, Reno, Nevada, December 19, 1962; and with Margaret Schneider Eikelberger, Sparks, Nevada, December 20, 1962; *Co-operative Colonist*, March, 1918, p. 2.

[55] Interviews with Mrs. Jess Vulgamore, Sparks, Nevada, December 20, 1962; and with Ernie Kormier, Sparks, Nevada, December 20, 1962.

[56] Interviews with Artie Riggle, Sparks, Nevada, December 21, 1960, and November 24, 1962.

[57] Interviews with Alex Baumann, Fallon, Nevada, September 3, 1962, and August 3, 1964; with Martha Baumann, Fallon, Nevada, November 12, 1962; and with Ernest L. Baumann, Fallon, Nevada, January 5, 1963; *Co-operative Colonist*, August, 1916, p. 13.

[58] Interviews with Sam Hiibel, Fallon, Nevada, September 3, 1962, and January 5, 1963; and with Phillip Hiibel, Fallon, Nevada, August 3, 1964; Journal No. 6 in the McCarran Papers.

Chapter IV

Organization, Administration, and Politics

EGGLESTON CALLED the first stockholders meeting of the new Nevada Colony Corporation in A. Grant Miller's law office in Reno on May 1, 1916. Three stockholders were listed on the articles of incorporation, but since one of them, R. E. Bray, had returned to Missouri to sell his printing business, only W. I. DeLong and L. V. Flowers remained to conduct the meeting. As the only company stockholders present, DeLong and Flowers first adopted a code of by-laws and then opened the subscription books for new members. Attorney Miller, his wife Ethel, and Justus Taylor, a local postman and active socialist, subscribed for shares. The five stockholders elected themselves directors of the new company, convened a board of directors' meeting, chose Miller as president, and adopted a "Declaration of Purposes" which became the basic guideline followed throughout the life of the colony.

BOLD PLANS AND EARLY PROGRESS

The objectives of the Nevada Colony Corporation were to establish a series of cooperative communities which would specialize in agriculture, stock raising, and manufacturing, and which would become a major economic and political force in the state. The sale of stock and bonds would provide the necessary capital. All stock was to be sold at one dollar per share. One share represented one vote in stockholder meetings, but no shareholder could cast more than twenty-five hundred votes. Members of the organization were to be at one and the same time stockholders, employees of the company, and colonists. They also had to be Caucasian, at least eighteen years of age, and the owner of one thousand shares or more of capital stock before they would be accepted in the colony. As employees they would receive four dollars for an eight-hour day. At least one dollar of each day's labor was to be used for the purchase of additional stock until the colonist held twenty-five hundred shares. Sixty cents from each four dollars was to be paid in cash to the colonist. The remaining two dollars and forty cents was to accrue to the personal credit of the worker and would be paid on a pro rata basis from profits at the end of each year.

Every colonist, including children under eighteen years of age, received free food and shelter as long as the stockholder was an employee. Other necessities as well as luxuries were to be sold at cost at a company commissary. Hospitals, laundries, libraries, assembly halls, auditoriums, schools, theaters, and places for amusement were to be established for the use of all members. Furthermore, the corporation was obligated to support all colonists and their wives and children during periods of sickness, physical disability, or any incapacity due to injury or old age.[1]

The May 1 meeting agreed to grant C. V. Eggleston of the Union Security Company a contract whereby he would become the financial agent and sales manager. Eggleston's company was to handle all purchases and sales of real estate, capital stock, livestock, merchandise, machinery, and so on. All the advertising, printing, postage, travel costs, office personnel, and employment of sales agents was to be financed by the Union Security Company, for which it would receive 25 percent of all cash and property given in payment for colony stock not to exceed $250 for any one sale. The contract was for two years or until the five million shares of capital stock were sold.

After the arrangement was adopted, Eggleston made his first report to the colony. He presented them with 238.5 acres of land in Lassen County, California, and 780 acres in Churchill County, Nevada. Although Churchill County newspapers had indicated that fifteen ranchers had joined the colony, only seven had signed real estate agreements with Eggleston by May 1, 1916.[2] Six of the seven were not only Socialists, but had been candidates for local office on the Socialist ticket. Much of the land was mortgaged, and in a few instances second mortgages or tax liens confused the negotiations. Actually, little land was purchased outright but instead was leased with an option to buy. In several instances the owner had mortgaged the property to the Union Security Company in exchange for capital stock in the Nevada Colony Corporation. In addition to real estate, Eggleston produced a lengthy list of personal property which had been exchanged for colony stock or mortgaged by the owner so that he could buy stock.[3] The entire May 1 transaction was valued at 53,550 shares. The stock was issued to Eggleston for transferal to the new colonists. As fiscal agent, the Union Security Company retained a sizeable block of Nevada Colony Corporation stock and also held two second mortgages which were to insure the payment of its commissions.

In the last major action of the organizational meeting, Ethel Miller resigned as vice-president and director, and Eggleston, who as a result of his commissions had become the largest stockholder in the company, was elevated to the board and replaced Ethel Miller as vice-president.

In mid-May, the company was confronted by a demand from four Lassen County ranchers that their land be returned. They insisted that it had been conveyed to Harriman and the old Nevada Colony Corporation and not to Eggleston's new organization. Not wishing to become involved in a legal battle which would damage the company's reputation, it was agreed that the Union Security Company should negotiate the return of the 238.5 acres of California land. The loss seemed insignificant when compared with the Churchill County gains.

However, in his eagerness to secure the control of property, Eggleston involved the company in financial obligations and entanglements which resulted in a maze of litigation. Typical of the muddled transactions was the J. J. Wood affair. As one of the first Fallon ranchers to support the experiment, Wood transferred to the Nevada Colony Corporation twenty-six head of cattle, four horses, twenty-five hogs, fifty chickens, eight tons of hay plus harness, scrapers, wagons, dairy implements, and farm tools. In addition, Wood granted the company a $4,000 mortgage on his eighty acres located about five miles southeast of Hazen. In return, the company agreed to pay mortgages against the land and liens against the livestock totaling $3,453.91 and also to assume personal debts totaling $402.95. Finally, the company gave Wood 3,000 shares in capital stock and promised to pay him $592 in cash. About a year later, when Eggleston demanded his (the Union Security Company's) commission for the transaction, the Nevada Colony Corporation sold the $4,000 mortgage to Eggleston's wife Ella for $10 in lieu of giving him money or company stock. Obviously Wood could not pay the $4,000 mortgage so Eggleston foreclosed and moved onto the Wood ranch. Two years later, after further litigation, Wood was able to reclaim part of his livestock and tools from the Nevada Colony Corporation since it had failed to pay off the original liens.[4]

Despite the confusing negotiations and Eggleston's willingness to purchase only a half interest in range land, city lots, and even livestock, the colony holdings were doubled during the summer of 1916. By September, 1916, some fifteen local landowners had granted the colony about 1,540 acres of Churchill County land plus two Fallon lots and an impressive list of livestock, farm machinery, and other personal property.[5] Capital stock had been traded for other lots at Sparks and Lake Tahoe, and in California. By the autumn of 1916, most of the real estate negotiations had been concluded.

Although widely scattered throughout the county, the property fell into three geographical districts. Some 480 acres were located in the Humboldt Sink area about thirty-two miles north of Fallon. The ranch which belonged to H. C. Taylor lay astride the main line of the Southern Pacific Railroad near Ocala and was wedged between the Carson and the Humboldt sinks. Two small frame buildings were constructed to supplement the living quarters provided by the old ranch house. Three hundred and twenty acres of extremely fertile soil known as the Sifford or Lower Ranch were located twelve miles northeast of Fallon near Stillwater. The permanent ranch house became the Lower Ranch Hotel, and by late 1917, two additional frame houses had been completed nearby. The 220 acres to be designated Nevada City lay along the Lincoln Highway (now U.S. 50) four miles east of Fallon. The remaining plots were scattered throughout the valley but most lay within a radius of three miles of Nevada City. Although colonists were located on most of the ranches, the headquarters was the Harmon ranch house, which was known as the Nevada City Hotel. Directly across the Lincoln Highway to the north of the hotel, five or six temporary frame houses were constructed in 1916 and early 1917. About one hundred yards southeast of the hotel, eight more unfinished lumber "cottages" were built in the same period. During the summer and autumn of 1917, a tent city grew up around the wooden buildings. On a slightly elevated area one-quarter mile south of the hotel, the permanent Nevada City was started in October, 1917. By early 1918, eight adobe and four frame dwellings had been completed and the foundation laid for a large hotel–community center.

Although several colonists settled at the Harmon ranch during the summer of 1916, Eggleston grew impatient for greater activity. Recognizing that most who wished to buy stock did not have the necessary $1,000, he initiated the installment system whereby the prospective colonist paid as little as $10 per month into the society. The installment member was not accepted as a resident, however, until the full payment of $1,000 was made. With fewer than twenty installment members by August, 1916, Eggleston advertised a system of special rates which allowed single men to be admitted for $250 and married persons for $500. An additional $100 was required for each child.[6]

The changes in admission fees were made without consultation with the board. Indeed, few of the directors appeared at scheduled meetings. Miller devoted most of his time to the campaign for the United States Senate; Flowers was often out of the state, and Justus Taylor had lost interest in the entire enterprise. At board meetings the directors automatically approved the policies of the general manager. Even when Eggleston informed the board that the company owed him $3,400 in commissions, no one asked for an itemized report. Instead, they expressed satisfaction that the claim was assigned to young E. G. Eggleston, who prepared a note at 8 percent interest and secured the debt by a chattel mortgage on 400 tons of colony hay.

INTERNAL DISSENSION

It was not until the first annual stockholders meeting held at Nevada City on November 14, 1916, that the directors became aware of the mounting dissatisfaction. Of the forty-seven stockholders present approximately twenty-five were longtime residents of the Fallon area and an additional five were Sparks socialists who had either traded property for shares or purchased stock outright. Most of the twenty-seven stockholders who were absent were installment members. A small group expressed immediate hostility to company policy. J. H. Barkley, leader of the dissident element, accused Eggleston of false advertising and misrepresentation of colony facilities; he ended a harangue by demanding the resignation of all the directors. After much wrangling all factions agreed on a slate of candidates. In the election which followed, Eggleston and DeLong received the largest number of votes, but Miller, Justus Taylor, and Flowers were replaced by three local landowners who had conveyed their property to the colony. J. J. Wood, James Ahern, and H. C. Taylor were eventually seated as the new directors, but violence was narrowly averted when Fred Sander, former Socialist candidate for sheriff and onetime editor of the *Ballot Box*, was replaced as an election teller.[7]

Until the November election all board of directors' meetings had been conducted in Miller's Reno office. But the new board selected the Socialist headquarters in Fallon for their meeting room. Despite the earlier disagreements the new directors expressed complete confidence in Eggleston and followed his suggestions in facing a number of serious issues.

The most pressing problem confronting the new board was the demand by several installment members for the refund of their investment. Fred Mutschler of California had paid five hundred dollars into the colony on October 17, but upon learning of the dissension withdrew his application and started legal proceedings for the return of the money. The board decided to refund the five hundred dollars to prevent adverse publicity, but at the same time they determined to rid the colony of the source of irritation. In a special Sunday meeting on November 17, they terminated the contract of J. H. Barkley, who had been the instigator of much discontent.

As one of the first persons to arrive at the society's Fallon headquarters, Barkley had been granted membership on June 1, 1916, after paying only thirty dollars. As a former preacher, storekeeper, newspaperman, and salesman, Barkley, Eggleston believed, would assist in local promotion and become one of the directors of the organization.[8] Active in socialist work and a vigorous salesman, Barkley had formed the Uno Homo Fraternity at Madras, Oregon, where he was known as a "rank socialist" who had "the faculty of persuading others to furnish the capital while he furnished the ideas or schemes...."[9] However, Eggleston and Barkley soon quarreled, and the latter became one of the severest critics of the Eggleston policies.

Nevertheless, the expulsion of a fellow colonist revealed for the first time the uniquely powerful position of the board of directors. In canceling a contract they not only dismissed an employee from his work but they barred a cooperator from the occupancy of a house, alienated him from his friends and colleagues, canceled his accrued labor credits, and without legal action or compensation rendered valueless his shares in a corporation. Technically, the ejected colonist had the right to sell his stock, but the directors could bar the entry of the purchaser if they wished. Later, they announced that they would disapprove the application of such secondhand stock buyers.

Barkley's dismissal aroused bitter resentment, and on November 28, four more stockholders were expelled because they "in various ways worked detrimental to the interest of the colony."[10] One of the four, Artie B. Riggle, was the highly respected Socialist leader of Sparks, and another, Wallace G. Barker, was one of the seven original ranchers who exchanged his land for stock in the society. On the local scene, the colony's favorable image collapsed with the crisis of November, 1916.

For some four months Eggleston remained in complete control of the board. The new members seemed little concerned with colony policy; on at least five occasions in January and early February a quorum could not be secured to conduct necessary business. In late February, 1917, however, DeLong's objectivity as secretary was challenged, and ultimately all minutes were recorded and read before the adjournment of a meeting. When Eggleston presented a new contract under which his Union Security Company would receive 50 percent of all cash income from the sale of stock, Ahern and Wood objected. Thereupon, Eggleston amended the request so that he would not receive more than one hundred dollars on any one sale. But his motives were obvious. Since scores of installment accounts were opened only to be discontinued within a few months, he hoped to seize a larger share of the first payments. Eggleston precipitated the second major colony crisis by forcing the new contract through the board with a three-to-two vote.

The new contract aroused much animosity in the colony as well as among the directors, and in an effort to gain prestige and voting power, Eggleston asked that the board be expanded to seven members. Wood and Ahern agreed but demanded that the stockholders elect the two additional board members. They were outmaneuvered, and Eggleston and DeLong, with the help of H. C. Taylor, elevated Marle Woodson and Fred Sander to the newly created positions. The new directors had been handpicked several days before and upon their selection were waiting in the building ready to take the oath of office. As a Fallon rancher since 1907, Sander had played a dynamic role in the local Socialist party and had been among the first to lease his property to the colony. Woodson arrived at the colony in December, 1916, from Stillwater, Oklahoma. As former president of the Connell State Agricultural School, he was well informed, intelligent and persuasive, and an ardent supporter of Eggleston's policies.[11]

Woodson reorganized the labor force, placed foremen in charge of major departments, and made Sander farm superintendent in charge of all production. As chairman of a committee to report on the financial status of the colony, Woodson presented an impressive document which vindicated Eggleston's arrangements and ended with the injunction that "each colonist from now on, instead of raising Hell, start at once to raising something to eat and wear; kick but be sure that each kick is a boost for progress and harmony."[12]

Woodson clearly and specifically outlined the duties of every officer in the entire colony and devised a weekly time report and a monthly time schedule form to be kept and approved by appropriate foremen, the farm superintendent, and the colony manager. Eggleston gained further prestige when, in the early spring of 1917, H. L. Carnahan, the California commissioner of corporations who had forced Harriman to incorporate Llano in Nevada, accepted an appointment as California's resident agent and attorney for the Nevada Colony Corporation. Full privileges to sell the company stock were granted in California, and L. V. Flowers was installed in Oakland to oversee all California sales. The colony building program received renewed emphasis, a second newspaper was launched, and company automobiles were provided for the farm superintendent and colony doctor. Eggleston and Woodson were appointed as a committee to settle complaints arising from stockholders leaving the society. Occasionally, contracts were canceled outright, but in most instances arrangements were made whereby incoming colonists could purchase stock from those leaving.

Throughout most of March and April, 1917, Eggleston was absent on an advertising mission in the Midwest, and while he was away, colony opposition to his policies tended to solidify. In a meeting on May 7, Ahern and three colleagues forced through a resolution which called for Eggleston's and DeLong's resignations. The Nevada Colony Corporation would pay Eggleston's Union Security Company $10,500 for the cancellation of all agreements between the two companies. In devising a schedule for settlement, Eggleston received $4,925 in cash and the colony's interest in J. J. Wood's eighty-acre farm, along with its horses, hogs, chickens, wagons, hay, and dairy equipment. All livestock not specifically identified were to be selected by Eggleston from colony property. In addition, Eggleston was granted a $6,500 mortgage on all company real estate until the $4,925 cash payment could be made.[13]

Despite the decision of May 7, Eggleston and DeLong did not immediately resign from the board of directors; rather, on May 12 they forced through numerous "lame duck" measures. Two thousand shares of Eggleston's personal stock were transferred to R. E. Bray so that Bray might gain a full membership in the community. A colony lot in Oakland was given to Myrtle D. Flowers, wife of L. V. Flowers, in exchange for eight hundred shares of Eggleston's stock. DeLong was not only allowed to sell his stock at par but was assured that the company would assist in the payment of his personal utility bills in Fallon. In exchange for these unusual courtesies, Eggleston agreed to transfer both the printing plant and the subscription list of the *Cooperative Colonist* to R. E. Bray, who became the new editor. DeLong's resignation became effective May 14, and

Eggleston finally quit the board on June 12, 1917. Eggleston moved to the Wood ranch some twelve miles northwest of Fallon but was unable to collect most of the property guaranteed to the Union Security Company.

THE BRAY ADMINISTRATION

With the resignation of Eggleston and DeLong the board was reconstituted with five members, but Woodson and Sanders were quickly forced out; H. C. Taylor, a third Eggleston supporter, soon moved to California. With only two or three members of the board functioning, R. E. Bray, as head of publications and correspondence, emerged as the most influential man in the colony. Bray and the "rump" board initiated an energetic expansion program. Phil Wagner, managing editor of the *Social Revolution* of St. Louis, was called to Fallon and accepted the post of colony publicity director. Anyone interested in selling stock could be designated an agent and receive 5 percent on all shares sold.

Before leaving office, Woodson had outlined an ambitious bond drive. The new board made only slight modifications in the plan and appointed the Girard newspaperman, E. N. Richardson, to head a department in which he would receive 10 percent of the face value of all debentures sold. The first fifty thousand dollars was to be used to pay off all company indebtedness. Further sales would provide for the purchase and leveling of land and for colony expansion. A flour mill, a creamery, an overall factory, and other processing and industrial plants were to follow. All profits from the projects were to be deposited in a company sinking fund which would pay off the bonded indebtedness. The board authorized the sale of one hundred thousand dollars in coupon bonds with interest at 6 percent payable semi-annually. The first ten thousand dollars was to mature on January 1, 1928, and an additional ten thousand dollars on each January 1 thereafter. The bond holders were given a first lien on all company property, both real and personal.[14]

The new board also revamped the colony entrance fees. Eggleston's stock-selling program had been slipshod and inconsistent. The special rate of $250 allowed to single men was discontinued; after October 1, 1917, the fee was $750 for single persons and $1000 for families. Also after October 1, food was no longer provided free. A record of all withdrawals was kept at the commissary and the sum deducted from earned labor credits. Single persons eating at the hotels were charged a flat rate of thirty cents per meal, which was also deducted from the individual's labor credits.

In October, 1917, Bray became secretary for the board, and in November he was elected a director; however, he had for some months been a one-man force directing the legal, administrative, and social life of the colony. He moved the company headquarters from Reno to Fallon and the location for the board meetings from Fallon to Nevada City. Bray initiated proceedings to establish a post office in the community. He purchased the equipment and set up a filling station for both colony and public use, and he started construction of the permanent adobe brick houses on Euclid Avenue. In October, 1917, agricultural production almost paid current colony expenses, thereby allowing entrance fees to be directed into the building program and the paying off of mortgages.[15] An irrigation program at the Humboldt ranch resulted in the completion of a mile of major canal, plus considerable clearing of brush and leveling for alfalfa.

Extensive leveling, ditching, fall plowing, and a sensible plan for planting and seeding was underway at the Lower Ranch. At Nevada City leaders stressed hard work instead of socialist theory. Plans for making Churchill County into the cooperative center of the United States or for carrying the state for socialism had been abandoned as had the idea that the colony must be large to be successful. The ruinous arrangement whereby the Union Security Company seized a large share of all membership fees and misrepresented the colony in an effort to make sales had been discontinued. Even the contract whereby Richardson received 10 percent for selling the company bonds quickly came under attack and was soon canceled.

But despite the encouraging trends, the unusually large influx of new members emphasized one of the colony's major deficiencies. Two-thirds of the migrants were without adequate housing, and sanitary conditions were appalling. During the winter of 1917–1918, three children died, and a dozen others became ill with pneumonia and typhoid. A second problem was the arrangement with Eggleston. As a result of mounting pressure, the directors renounced the agreements of May and June and employed attorneys to force the return of company property held by the Union Security Company. But issues became confused by claims and counterclaims, and Eggleston's friends in Fallon, and even a few colonists, worked for the defeat of the new management.

Another problem was the shortage of food. In the winter of 1916–1917, few out-of-state cooperators had arrived at the colony, and the society was able to draw on the large quantities of food and stock feed provided by the Fallon ranchers who had become members. During the winter of

1917–1918, the colony numbered approximately two hundred active members, and the surplus stores had been exhausted. Furthermore, local farmers, who formed the backbone of early colony life, had become estranged from the organization by the winter of 1917–1918.

The policy of withdrawing the working contract from dissident elements had long been an all too frequent method by which the management attempted to silence opposition. But in November and December, 1917, Bray introduced the "reign of terror." On November 7 the board met in special session, and Secretary Bray submitted a list of thirty-three stockholders whose working contracts were up for cancellation. Former directors and landowners like Fred Sander and H. C. Taylor, property owners like Henry C. Taylor, Jr. and J. S. Harmon, the Sparks Socialist and businessman Jud Harris, and W. I. DeLong were included on Bray's list. Even one of the absent directors, H. S. Baker, was voted out of the colony. Adolph Baumann and his five stockholding children were all expelled.

In some instances expulsion was a mere formality as the colonists had already left Nevada City, but in the case of the Baumanns, Bray employed attorneys to gain possession of property which the family had allegedly agreed to turn over to the colony.[16] It was a striking paradox. The Baumanns were forced from the colony thereby losing their investment in it; yet at the same time, legal action was initiated which would have required them to invest further in a company from which they had been excluded. Truly, the colony had lost sight of its original objective to promote communal tranquility and end capitalistic exploitation.

At the second annual stockholders meeting held on November 13, 1917, a committee headed by Secretary Bray proposed a revamping of company bylaws. According to the Bray formula the secretary would be granted more power, the board would again be expanded to seven members, and each director would file a letter of resignation before taking the oath of office. Any policy approved either by a vote of the stockholders or at a colony meeting was to be affirmed by the directors. If any board member failed to support the popularly approved program, the secretary was to record the date on the standing resignation, and the obstinate director was thereby removed. Any possible colony opposition had been silenced by the canceling of thirty-three contracts six days earlier. Since Bray held the proxies of the installment members, the bylaw changes were routinely endorsed.

Bray had engineered the formation of instant democracy in which a day to day popularity poll became the sole criterion for remaining in office. From all power for the directorate under Eggleston's administration, the policy had shifted to immediate power for the people.[17] A simple majority of those holding working permits in the colony could command the vote or resignation of any director. Furthermore, in broadening the base for the grass-roots democracy, all members of families holding working contracts, including wives and children over eighteen years of age, were given the vote. Proxies were not recognized at local meetings, and many colonists worked miles from Nevada City and seldom participated in the community politics. Therefore, it only remained for Bray to assume the role of benefactor while ruthlessly eliminating dissent, and the rule of the demagogue would be inaugurated.

Meanwhile, the purge of dissident socialists continued. In late November, George Thompson, the Nevada City hotelkeeper and Bray's assistant in proposing the bylaw changes of November 13, fell into disfavor and was dismissed. Indeed, during November and December, 1917, a total of forty-five stockholders were excluded from further participation in the colony. James Ahern, the last Fallon rancher associated with the experiment and a member of the board of directors, pointed out the illogic and injustice of such behavior, but his pleas were ignored.

Although elected to the board of directors on November 13, Bray submitted his resignation some two weeks later. The action was not designed to weaken his influence. Actually, he had become deeply involved in colony finances and hoped to avoid criticism by claiming no authority. Bray's son, Ralph, operated the printing plant; his wife, Lillian, served for several months as company bookkeeper, and after presenting a bill for four hundred dollars, the directors had given her the Weigel lot in the Oats Park district of Fallon. In exchange for the payment of taxes and other pressing obligations, Bray held two mortgages against colony property. His resignation from the directorate did not weaken his influence. Indeed, he retained control and yet escaped accountability for his policies.

Minutes of colony meetings were not kept, or at least not preserved, after January 1, 1918, but there were few official sessions to report. Although Nevada City struggled on for sixteen months, it could not regain the enthusiasm of its first exciting weeks. The directors had set the stage for disintegration by alternatively packing and reducing the size of the board, by canceling the working contracts of some three score members, and by giving instant and total power to the colonists. In late January, the new president of the board, H. C. Power, a former merchant of Post,

Texas, and Secretary Bray clashed in a struggle for control. For some two months they waged a childish popularity campaign, but Power eventually moved to Fallon and became the proprietor of a pool hall. The exodus of Power and his friends reduced the colony to some twenty-five stockholders, but Bray, rather pleased with his personal victory, again reorganized the board and appointed C. V. Carithers, an Idaho farmer, as the new president. Continuing in the policy of excluding opponents, the reconstituted board, on April 27, canceled the contracts of Power and five of his supporters.[18] Bray's success, however, was short-lived.

Convinced that he combined the qualities of a reform politician, a crusading editor, and a frontier philosopher, Bray brushed aside all criticism as the product of jealous and unimaginative detractors. He had for years practiced a freewheeling, extempore brand of journalistic promotion in which the opposition was labeled the "Van Buren gang." This sobriquet for his Fallon critics derived from Bray's questionable schemes and his being asked to leave Hunter, Missouri, by officials at the nearby county seat of Van Buren. The phrase became even more meaningful when James Partney, a Missouri antagonist, joined the colony in March, 1918, thus transferring an Ozark feud to the Lahonton Valley. Although careful in organization, pleasant in demeanor, and conservative in taste, Bray had devoted most of his life to the support of transitory causes in which he invariably alienated friendly supporters.

During the spring of 1918, Bray exerted every effort trying to rebuild the community. The *Co-operative Colonist* advertised for specialists like bakers, barbers, carpenters, and bricklayers. To further emphasize the local control, the colony office was moved from Fallon to Nevada City and located in the rear of the commissary. The board voted an increase in wages from four to five dollars per day and promised an expansion of commissary facilities. Nevertheless, adverse publicity and the war rapidly dried up the earlier stream of new arrivals, and most of those who did request membership were old, disabled, or women seeking a retirement home. During May the directors debated the advisability of discontinuing stock sales. In a letter of June 6, 1918, the federal government decided the issue for them. The War Finance Corporation Act of April 5, 1918, authorized a committee to determine whether the sale of securities in excess of one hundred thousand dollars by any corporation was in the national interest.[19] If the colony wished to continue selling stock, the government would demand a thorough accounting of the company's activities and conduct an investigation. The directors agreed to terminate all stock sales as of July 1, 1918.

As a lawyer Bray recognized the impossibility of contesting all the suits being brought against the colony. Furthermore, he had arrived at Nevada City more than a year after the first negotiations had been completed. He was constantly shocked by financial and legal demands of which he knew nothing. For example, he discovered that the colony had neither a map nor an accurate survey of the Humboldt property. Not only had the much publicized irrigation canal been improperly planned but there had been no investigation of the water rights. In short, a ditch was dug on someone else's property to carry water which did not exist in a canal which ran uphill. The futile attempt to maintain possession of the G. B. Seifling farm at the southeast edge of Fallon further pointed up the hopelessness of the situation. The Seifling agreements were found to be so complicated that attorneys for both parties readily ad-. mitted their inability even to summarize the facts.

Meanwhile, as more colonists left or were forced from the society, an alliance of outsiders formed at Fallon. James Ahern, who had finally deserted the colony in January, 1918, signed affidavits attesting to the accuracy of the critical pamphlet circulated by J. H. Barkley in December, 1916. George L. Thompson, whom Bray expelled in November, 1917, appeared along with several others at a hearing in Fallon to testify that the colony was a swindle. Even such unlikely ex-colonists as Barkley, Eggleston, Ahern, and Power joined forces. As the first person to be expelled from Nevada City, Barkley longed for the society's collapse. With mortgages entitling him to considerable property, Eggleston now worked for the colony's demise. Ahern, H. C. Taylor, the Baumanns, and Fred Sander hoped that they might be able to regain their ranches. H. C. Power, R. B. Ellis, and others had become embittered by Bray's high-handed methods. Most were delighted with the Lahonton Valley and wanted the colony out of the way so that they could start a new life in the area.

In late May the "Van Buren group" at Fallon attempted to force a stockholders meeting at which time they hoped to gain control. Bray, however, quickly alerted the colonists and amassed proxies from installment members; consequently, the plan collapsed. With the confusing legal web tightening about the society, Bray determined to hold only the Harmon ranches at Nevada City and at Stillwater and allow the other land to be claimed by court order. The whole colony idea was collapsing so rapidly, however, that he began to lose interest. In June he wrote to a friend, "why keep up a losing fight? The war has hit us so hard that we do not feel perfectly able to put the colony over the top."[20] Two months later he asked his Oklahoma colleague, Elijah Opdyke, to assume the post of secretary, and before issuing the September and last number of the *Co-operative Colonist*, he laid the groundwork for his departure.

On October 1, 1918, C. E. Maxwell of Batesville, Arkansas, arrived at Nevada City. Bray sold Maxwell his personal stock and during October transferred labor credits and other possessions to the new arrival. The autumn harvest provided the company with sufficient cash to pay off two notes held by Bray, and on October 31, 1918, the colony paid eight dollars to finance his move to Fallon.[21] Bray proceeded to Washington, D.C., where he secured a job with a printing firm. The family followed within a few weeks.

THE UNITED DEVELOPMENT COMPANY

In September, president Carithers' son died at Ft. Lewis, Washington. The family hastened to their old home at Moscow, Idaho, for the burial and failed to return to Nevada City. Secretary Opdyke, Dr. A. C. Adams, and Dr. B. F. Harrison, all of Oklahoma, maintained only a rough semblance of leadership during the winter of 1918–1919. Many of the settlers filed suit against the colony, but when offered livestock, machinery, or grain they quickly agreed to a compromise. The commissary remained open, however, and colonists continued to accrue work credits and earn additional shares in the company.

On April 1, 1919, eleven stockholders remained at Nevada City, and C. V. Eggleston had again amassed sufficient strength to assume leadership of the colony. At a stockholders' meeting in early April, Eggleston engineered the election of H. C. Power as the new president and John M. Sovil of Florida as secretary of the rapidly collapsing organization. Through the efforts of Dr. Harrison, Maxwell, and Ahern, the new officers acquired the proxies for 114,841 of the 154,966 shares of outstanding stock. At a meeting of the board of directors called on April 30, the Nevada Colony Corporation reorganized as the United Development Company. The action was designed to delay legal proceedings against the colony and to reestablish the company as a purely business concern. The pendulum of control had swung from left to right; a truly capitalistic organization had finally emerged.

Power remained president and Sovil, secretary of the new company, but Eggleston became vice-president. The chief purpose of the United Development Company was the disposal of property and the handling of actions brought against the Nevada Colony Corporation. It also brought about the demise of Eggleston's Union Security Company, which had no further reason to exist. The farmland yet in company possession was leased to former colonists, while Power and Sovil employed themselves at two hundred dollars per month to function as executors of the estate. Claimants came forward, and negotiations and final settlement were often concluded within a few minutes. The colony owed N. C. Whitaker forty-eight dollars in cash credits. He accepted seven hives of bees. C. E. Maxwell presented a claim for five dollars and was handed six boxes of matches, six bottles of extract, sixteen bars of soap, four-dozen fruit jars, and the bill stamped paid. Plows, buggies, chairs, saddles, windfall apples, chickens, and sanitary closets were sold outright or offered as payment for colony debts. For a series of notes totaling more than five thousand dollars, Eggleston accepted the printing press and several pieces of farm machinery.[22] James Ahern bargained for the return of his farm; however, like other ranches it had been mortgaged to the I. H. Kent mercantile company in return for colony supplies.

Obviously, all property settlements could not be effected through the exchange of soap and matches. Although Adolph Baumann in June, 1922, won a suit against the United Development Company which assured the return of his farm, he was then forced to pay the I. H. Kent Company for mortgages incurred while the property was in the hands of the colony. As the last colonist to arrive at Nevada City, Frank R. Driskell was granted the company mortgage on the Arthur A. Baumann farm, and after extended litigation he forced its sale on August 1, 1921. Baumann repurchased the eighty acres after paying the judgment of $1481.88.[23] After a lawsuit, H. C. Taylor regained most of his land, but the Wallace G. Barker ranch was sold to the mortgagor for $618. In October, 1919, the colony's equity in the two Harmon ranches was sold to Tipton Depp for $500. During the winter of 1919–1920, Depp moved most of the frame houses to Fallon and removed the timbered roofs and window frames from the adobe buildings, leaving only bare walls to stand testimony to Nevada City. H. C. Power lived in the cement-block colony hotel until late 1919, but only three of the original fifteen property owners who helped to launch the colony were back on their land in January, 1920. Some ten of the more than one hundred stockholders who came to Nevada during the hectic three years settled permanently in the Lahonton Valley.[24]

It must be concluded that the founder and many of the

directors of the Nevada colony were activated by a mercenary and competitive spirit aimed at initiating a profitable business operation as well as at building a new social order. Throughout the colony's three years the real weakness was always from within and from above. Confused and unprincipled leaders defeated the call for sacrifice, and the steady drift into a semicapitalistic venture belied the claims of cooperation. For most participants as well as for most Nevada observers, group socialism emerged as a synonym for delusion and futility. It was, according to the Gardnerville *Record-Courier*, "a house of cards," a dream which must end in a "rude awakening."[25]

Yet, forty-five years later, a few of the colony members still insist that their society stood as a worthy ideal. They believe that above all their adventure offered men hope— hope for a union of production and consumption, for combining agriculture, industry, and handicrafts, and for harmonizing the conflict between ethical behavior and capitalistic competition.

NOTES

[1] Minute Book of the McCarran Papers in the Nevada Historical Society, Reno. See attachment to p. 10.

[2] The seven original ranchers to sign real estate agreements were James and Alice Ahern, Wallace G. and Kate Barker, Adolph and Martha Baumann, Arthur A. Baumann, J. S. and Naomi Harmon, Fred C. and Charity Sander, and H. C. and Nancy Taylor.

[3] A list of the property included 2 stallions, 35 horses, 37 cows, 2 bulls, 16 heifers, 7 steers, 220 hogs, 142 chickens, 24 turkeys plus a threshing machine, 2 plows, 2 mowers, harrows, disks, derricks, hay rakes and other machinery, farm implements and hand tools. Minute Book of the McCarran Papers. See attachment to p. 9.

[4] Office of the Recorder, Churchill County, Nevada. *Mortgages,* IV, 544; *Miscellaneous,* XI, 144; *Assignments and Releases,* II, 308–310 and XI, 53. Also see p. 29 in Minute Book of the McCarran Papers.

[5] In addition to agreements with the seven original ranch owners, contracts were signed with F. A. Austin, J. J. Wood, N. C. Whitaker, William H. Bowman, C. B. Serfling, G. P. Weigel, William H. Lowry, and W. R. Streeper.

[6] *Co-operative Colonist* (Fallon), August, 1917, p. 7.

[7] Minute Book of the McCarran Papers, pp. 43–47.

[8] Colony Agreements in the McCarran Papers.

[9] County Clerk, Jefferson County, Oregon, to L. V. Flowers, January 25, 1917, in Miscellaneous No. 6 of the McCarran Papers.

[10] Minute Book of the McCarran Papers, p. 57.

[11] For a brief report on Fred C. Sander see *Nevada Colony News* (Fallon), April, 1917, p. 6. For a discussion of Marle Woodson's activities see *Nevada Colony News,* April, 1917, p. 7.

[12] Minute Book of the McCarran Papers, p. 77.

[13] *Ibid.,* p. 94.

[14] *Co-operative Colonist,* July, 1917, pp. 2 and 8; September, 1917, p. 3; October, 1917, p. 3.

[15] Cash Record Book, October and November, 1917, and Day Book No. 3, poultry income, of the McCarran Papers.

[16] Minute Book of the McCarran Papers, pp. 137–138.

[17] *Ibid.,* pp. 139–141.

[18] Colony Agreements in the McCarran Papers.

[19] California State Corporation Department to Nevada Colony Corporation, June 6, 1918, in Miscellaneous No. 6 of the McCarran Papers.

[20] R. E. Bray to Peter Husley, June 15, 1918, in Miscellaneous No. 7 of the McCarran Papers.

[21] Cash Record Book in the McCarran Papers.

[22] Journal No. 5 and Journal No. 6 in the McCarran Papers.

[23] Office of the Recorder, Churchill County, Nevada. *Miscellaneous,* XII, 401–481.

[24] The charter of the United Development Company was revoked on the first Monday in March, 1924, because of failure to pay a $10 corporation fee. See United Development Company, Office of the Secretary of State, Carson City, Nevada.

[25] *Record-Courier* (Gardnerville), May 30, 1919, p. 1, c. 3.

Chapter V

Economic Ambitions
and
Social Contrasts

MOST OF THE FAMILIES who were drawn to the Fallon colony had been touched by disappointment and discouraged "by the brutal principle of competition." Instead of moving forward, they seemed to be losing ground; life was unfolding in reverse. Somewhat alarmed, they could not avoid dreams of a time when the common sense of unsophisticated people would provide a sympathetic and productive society for all. In their desire to become a part of the future, they allowed their instinctive skepticism to be replaced by a naive faith; they eagerly overlooked the chasm between fact and fantasy. They could not exercise sufficient detachment to guard against being submerged by the vigorous and partisan appeal of the cooperative idea. After joining the colony, the gap between expectation and realization steadily widened. Too often, when effort, intelligence, and unity were needed to bridge the gulf, a policy of drift ensued. The leaders from time to time tried to keep the colonists from becoming dispirited by suggesting further fantasies. But a myth can not long sustain when reality constantly belies it.

The construction of the permanent town at Nevada City typified the exaggeration and negligence of the colony management. The town, originally planned for the H. C. Taylor ranch, was given much publicity, but no actual attention, during Eggleston's tenure. Soon after Eggleston's resignation, a ten-acre tract lying one-quarter mile south of the Harmon farmhouse was set aside for the new city. Two colonists were appointed "architects" and a detailed and imaginative plan soon presented. Rattlesnake Hill, some two miles to the northwest, provided easily accessible quantities of lightweight volcanic basalt particularly suitable for the foundations. After weeks of experimentation a simple process was devised for molding bricks from the sandy soil. The bricks were inferior in quality, but at peak periods of production some 3,000 could be pressed and sunbaked in one day. Two streets were laid out, and construction of houses started in September, 1917. The two east-west traffic ways were some 96 feet in width with lots 100 feet wide by 120 feet deep staked out along either side. But before the first one-story, hip-roof, adobe house was completed, Bray began to advertise the second hundred units. A circular boulevard was to surround the ten acres with a park, tennis courts, croquet grounds, a ball park, flower gardens, walkways, and a sunken garden accessible from the thoroughfare. A road extending north from the colony would provide the approach to the Lincoln Highway. An impressive arch over the road was to direct travelers to the city, and a filling station and garage along the highway could become lucrative enterprises.

Only two streets, with eight adobe and four frame dwellings, became a reality at the townsite. Houses were designed with three and five rooms, but only one was expanded into a two-story structure. The telephones, electricity, sprinkling system, and running water were never installed. The hotel was planned on a scale befitting the new city, but only the foundation was completed. The main section of the hotel had a street frontage of 185 feet with three wings of 25 by 100 feet each extending to the rear. The wings were to house the library, the printing plant, and the assembly hall.[1] As director of construction, William Pierce at first showed considerable enthusiasm; in late 1917, however, he rejoined his family in St. Louis, and when he returned to Nevada City the following April, he had determined to become a prospector. Pierce eventually resettled at the colony and in July declared himself ready despite "slackers, pessimists and the war" to complete the hotel, but construction was not resumed.

Practically every economic undertaking advertised or pursued by the colony proved as illusory as the building of "adobe town." In August, 1917, the *Co-operative Colonist* announced that Jud Harris of Sparks had "turned over to the colony his mattress factory." Furthermore, Harris agreed to supervise the new industry which, with colony capital, was to be expanded to manufacture "couches, tables, chairs, ice chests, cupboards [and] clothes chests." Supposedly, the venture provided enough cabinets and upholstered furniture to meet current demands in the colony and was geared to supply Nevada mining communities and sell on the open market.[2] After much publicizing of the

Sparks industry, local colonists discovered that Harris operated a secondhand store and had never engaged in manufacturing. He had traded the property to the Union Security Company for colony stock and a two hundred-dollar personal note which Eggleston never paid.[3]

The colony's milling enterprise proved equally deceptive. On November 8, 1916, Eggleston traded F. W. Inman one thousand shares of capital stock for a flour mill and other machinery located about seven miles southeast of Nevada City. The mill, badly in need of repair, was never made operative by the colony. A Fallon carpentry shop proved to be a frame building only thirty by sixteen feet. Eggleston had traded sixty-five dollars worth of stock certificates for the rough shedlike structure.[4] A movie projector, electric fans, a heating system, a typewriter, and other secondhand equipment were also acquired in exchange for company stock.

A dozen promotional ventures undertaken as adjuncts to the regular community program were stillborn. The Funk and Wagnalls Company refused to furnish the society dictionaries in exchange for advertising space in the *Colonist*. Nor would the Zellerbach Paper Company, despite the large orders for both paper and ink, grant a discount or buy advertising in the colony paper. The "handsome profit" which the producers of Salome soap guaranteed the directors if they would purchase the product turned out to be only a modest discount. Edward E. Smith of Dallas, Texas, bought stock in and traveled to the colony with plans for a bluing and ink factory and a tannery, but the new industry never passed the advertising stage. Seventy-one-year-old Chard Lang of Longdale, Oklahoma, was to make Nevada City the home of an ointment-compound, guaranteed to cure "all kinds of ills," and Fred Jordon of Paducah, Kentucky, was to manufacture his hog and chicken remedy at the colony. However, in negotiating the details of the agreements it was found that neither Lang nor Jordon had sufficient funds to travel to Nevada.

Although the colony was granted the opportunity to retail hog feeders, it was denied the agency for Butterfly cream separators, for Goodyear tires, and for Albaugh-Dover tractors. Several insurance companies rejected the society's bid to become their Nevada agent. An ambitious scheme was devised with J. B. Jenkins of Paonia, Colorado, whereby the colony was to gain control of the retail coal business at Fallon. Jenkins traveled to Nevada in early 1917 and with DeLong worked out the details of the plan. The first coal shipments were scheduled for July, 1917, but the arrangements were terminated when Eggleston was forced from office in June.[5] At one point the directors traded for nine dozen riding quirts which were to be sold for one dollar each. But the socialist demand for riding quirts proved surprisingly limited. Several small capitalists investigated the colony with a view to utilizing its cheap and controlled manpower, and in at least one instance negotiations were undertaken, but no outside industry was established.

A pair of imported Percheron stallions, Marathon Junior and Julian, gained considerable publicity for the colony and won several prizes at shows and fairs, but they were a poor financial investment. Stud service for the spring of 1918 totaled only $270. The farm manager repeatedly recommended that the animals be sold, and in the meantime he made special collars for the stallions and used them as draft horses.[6] It was believed that the profits from a gasoline station and garage along the Lincoln Highway would be sufficient to supply the colony with its petroleum needs free of charge. Bray supervised the purchase of the station equipment from the Standard Oil Company and temporarily installed the gasoline pumps near the Harmon ranch house. The board of directors voted three financial grants to assist J. J. Wood to attend auto mechanics school in San Francisco. But by the time Wood returned to Nevada City in July, 1918, litigation and the seizure of colony property precluded the opening of the enterprise.

Despite numerous failures, the directors did promote several profitable economic arrangements. Marle Woodson, a former federal employee, completed an agreement with the United States Department of Agriculture whereby the government contracted to undertake experiments on twenty-two acres of colony land. All costs were borne by the federal agency and all produce turned over to the society. Agreements were also worked out with fruit growers and lumbermen whereby the colony received products in exchange for capital stock. In a few instances the products for which the directors paid nothing were resold by the colony at a handsome profit. The commissary was generally well supplied with California prunes, and the Nevada City ranches were furnished with hundreds of Washington fence posts at no cost to the society. The *Colonist* subscription list occasionally proved valuable. H. A. Prinegar of Wellington, Utah, exchanged thousands of raspberry plants for a mailing roster of some three thousand names, and during February, 1918, similar discussions were conducted with Upton Sinclair. In April, 1918, Sinclair undertook the publication of a periodical entitled *Upton Sinclair's* and later the same year he issued the book *The Profits of Religion*. Sinclair was understandably anxious to secure the colony's roster of socialist names and addresses, but Bray's curt letters and exorbitant demands led to a breaking off of the negotiations.[7]

Many of the colony leaders demonstrated a distinct penchant for becoming involved in ill-considered capitalistic enterprises. Clearly, the most opportunistic undertaking was the creation of the phosphate and the potash syndicates. In January, 1918, R. E. Bray, Fred Sander, Marle Woodson, and E. N. Richardson declared their intention to organize the Nevada Phosphate Syndicate. Sander and Woodson, supposedly bitter critics of Bray, had left the colony soon after Eggleston resigned. Richardson had been suspended as colony bond salesman in January, 1918. Nevertheless, Bray was welcomed into the enterprise and immediately undertook the selling of phosphate stock through normal colony channels. Although the enterprise was technically a private company, Bray linked it with the socialist society. Indeed, he assured prospective colonists that royalties from the mining activities would soon "put the society on easystreet." He combined phosphate advertisements with those of the colony in a dozen socialist papers, and the January and February, 1918, numbers of the *Co-operative Colonist* carried full page announcements of "one of the greatest phosphate fields in the world." Ten million tons of rock phosphate were to provide the production which could win the war. In fact, the company was "a bayonet thrust into the Kaiser's armour."[8] Within six weeks the promoters had sold two thousand dollars worth of pre-organization shares, but investigation by mineralogists revealed the worthlessness of the Humboldt Valley deposit.

Rather than return the money, all stock purchased in the

phosphate syndicate was transferred to a newly created potash syndicate. The *Churchill County Standard* in a front-page article lauded the promoters for their exceptional honesty and incorrectly explained that the two thousand dollars had been refunded. It further suggested that the Dixie Valley potash mines represented a good investment.[9] By April, 1918, all discussion of phosphate was dropped, and the *Co-operative Colonist* ran an article entitled "Potash Men Get Wealthy." The May and June numbers of the paper explained that English, French, and Russian companies were investing in California potash mines and would soon move on to Nevada. But despite the proclaimed wealth of the venture, Bray would not refund the earlier investments made in phosphate stock.[10] Most of the phosphate and potash stockholders were also installment members in the colony, and as a result of the mining chicanery, they came to suspect the entire cooperative program. Only the most dedicated and unsuspecting socialists remained unquestioning after the phosphate and potash fiasco.

Another generally unsatisfactory arrangement grew out of the trading of capital stock for property. Timber lands in Oregon, a farm in West Virginia, houses in California, and town lots in Oklahoma were inspected and often received as payment for company stock. Books, chairs, typewriters, lumber, food, livestock, machinery, and automobiles were also exchanged. Although the acceptance of private property often led to expensive legal involvements, it sometimes proved profitable. The 33 cattle sent from Kansas by Peter Hiibel and the 103 angora goats shipped from Bay View, Idaho, by O. A. Nickerson became valuable additions to the livestock holdings of the society. A certificate of questionable value on a Memphis building and loan association which was accepted as payment for a small colony bond was later found to be worth $1,030.

INCOME AND EXPENDITURES

Although many and varied economic programs were undertaken by the colony, it was the selling of capital stock, both by installment and to direct subscribers, which provided the society with its major income. During the community's first year of activity, the Union Security Company and Eggleston's private finances were so thoroughly intermingled with those of the colony that no effort was made to disassociate them. However, for the period April 23 through July 9, 1917, a partially destroyed ledger suggests a total colony income of $5,334.98. Disbursements for the same period totaled $5,505.45 of which $1,676.75 was paid to C. V. Eggleston and the Union Security Company for services rendered.[11]

Reasonably complete records reveal the company's sources of income during the last half of 1917 and the first months of 1918. Between October 1, 1917, and May 13, 1918, the colony sold about ten dozen eggs and some seventy gallons of milk per day. In one week in December, $264 worth of dressed pork plus more than $50 worth of sausage, hams, and lard was peddled to Fallon buyers. Corn, beans, tomatoes, pumpkins, sorghum, and ten thousand cabbages were sold during the autumn of 1917; receipts from apples, potatoes, and onions totaled $69.12 in January, 1918. But despite the proceeds from farm, poultry, and dairy products, it was the cash received from new memberships and install-

142

ment payments which formed the economic backbone of the organization. Between July 12 and September 27, 1917, 104 installment members and 11 new arrivals at Nevada City contributed $11,634 to the colony.[12] On one day in September, 12 new installment memberships were received. Total colony outlay for the same period was $12,355.70. The purchase of stock, therefore, paid nearly all colony disbursements during the summer of 1917 and by October was more than covering all expenses. The normal colony income from all sources, other than stock sales, was capable of supplying less than one quarter of the routine costs of operating the community (see tables 2 and 3).

An apparently complete file of check stubs for the period July 31, 1917, through January 3, 1919, provides an accurate picture of colony expenditures for almost a year and a half. In the five months, July 31 through December 31, 1917, 336 checks were issued totaling $27,707.17. The largest amount, $5,668.08, went for commissary supplies. More than $5,000 was devoted to the payment of mortgages, interest on notes, and taxes, and more than $3,600 was devoted to the purchase of building materials. Wages and the buying of agricultural equipment and livestock also accounted for large expenditures.

Many private obligations were assumed by the colony: for example, the bills for mail-order shipments from Sears Roebuck and Company were merely passed on to the management for payment. Subsequent deductions were made from the family's earned labor credits. Checks for personal lodge dues, mechanic fees for the repairing of private automobiles, and individual poll tax assessments were paid by the colony. Petty loans and advances from the company were commonplace. On December 24, 1917, nine stockholders

TABLE 2

COLONY INCOME[a]

Month	Poultry	Farm products	Dairy	Commis-sary	Printing	Payments from new members	Install. payments	Miscel-laneous[b]	Total
Oct., 1917	$134.50	$ 99.05	$347.16	$20.75	$136.94	$4560.00	$2045.00	$ 775.99	$8119.39
Nov., 1917	67.24	162.83	238.72	25.65	8.75	1000.00	660.00	1632.87	3796.06
Dec., 1917	36.23	500.98	167.95	49.00	39.26	1240.00	1200.00	1803.04	5036.46
Jan., 1918	27.42	69.12	262.85	8.10	92.13	2180.00	680.00	1572.24	4881.86
Feb., 1918	163.18	28.13	191.21	10.00	75.50	100.00	350.00	436.91	1354.93
Mar., 1918	27.00	16.10	152.30	0	76.00	680.00	555.50	186.25	1693.15
Apr., 1918	37.91	24.33	87.32	36.00	152.25	240.00	440.00	20.53	1038.31
May, 1918[c]	83.87	?	91.75	0	27.76	240.00	1000.00	61.50	1504.88

[a] Detailed records have been preserved for a period of seven and one-half months, only.
[b] Most of the miscellaneous income was from the sale of bonds.
[c] The May figures include only the period May 1 through 13.

TABLE 3

COLONY EXPENDITURES[a]

Month	Labor fees to colonists	Commissary	Building	Petty cash	Equipment, feed, and seed	Mortgages, interest, old bills	Commission on bonds	Miscellaneous	Total
Oct., 1917 . .	$991.75	$1416.40	$1069.40	$ 48.00	$ 135.64	$1995.65	$ 40.50	$815.75	$6512.97
Nov., 1917 .	813.14	1492.94	627.85	47.44	313.55	19.50	154.50	797.94	4266.86
Dec., 1917 .	595.66	980.50	1287.36	49.00	1057.07	200.00	102.50	563.96	4836.05
Jan., 1918 . .	640.00	379.78	1216.53	89.30	265.87	0	111.37	522.50	3225.35
Feb., 1918 . .	363.81	168.33	472.32	96.70	645.92	50.00	0	274.82	2071.90
Mar., 1918 .	66.70	367.50	550.00	100.00	254.97	50.00	0	24.50	1413.67
Apr., 1918 . .	101.90	79.12	0	0	91.92	588.00	0	49.00	809.94
May, 1918[b] .	0	75.36	100.00	5.00	457.45	400.00	0	210.89	1248.70

[a] Detailed records have been preserved for a period of seven and one-half months, only.
[b] The May figures include only the period May 1 through 13.

were issued Christmas checks irrespective of their accrued labor credits. Fees were paid to a practical nurse for helping to take care of single men when they became ill, and when an entire family was stricken with typhoid fever, a colony lady received $3.50 per day for assisting the family until the adults had recovered. In short, the management diverted most of the colony income into the purchase of essentials, but did not overlook the personal problems of needy co-operators. Of the 193 checks totaling $11,985.02 written between January 1 and June 30, 1918, the pattern of expenditures changed little. During the last six months of 1918, only $7,286.47 worth of checks was written and almost half went for mortgage payments, interest, taxes, and insurance. The purchase of building materials had been discontinued.[13]

The value of supplies procured at the commissary by colony families varied greatly. In a few instances the value of goods obtained even exceeded the $2.40 accrued to the stockholder for each day worked. In the winter months, fuel as well as food and incidentals was deducted from the labor credit, and sickness and inclement weather often reduced the number of days worked. In December, 1917, the commissary bill for the Robert Ellis family of nine persons totaled $78.43. This amount was more than double the commissary credit accrued by Ellis in the same month.[14] On the other hand, in November, 1917, Dr. F. B. Harrison as a single man made only eleven purchases at the commissary. His total monthly charge was $1.15 plus ninety cents per day levied by the hotel for his meals.[15] The marked discrepancy between the needs of a single man and a family man tended to prompt the young and active to leave the colony, while men with large families or those who were sick or disabled tended to remain.

Sales at the commissary did not reflect the antitobacco movement. Ten of Dr. Harrison's eleven purchases of November, 1917, were for tobacco. Indeed, 25 percent of all nonfood sales were for tobacco; a corncob pipe cost five cents, and the popular plug of chewing tobacco sold for ten cents. Brooms, lamp globes, stovepipes, pencils, canning jars, toothpicks, sole leather, and pills were frequent purchases. Dried prunes and cornmeal, while not popular items, nevertheless, were the staples in the colony diet. The commissary even contributed to a steadily growing interest in private ownership. By November, 1917, individual members within the colony owned twelve automobiles. A touring club was organized, and the motorists secured their gasoline through the commissary. In a few instances the largest monthly charge against a stockholder's labor credits was not for food but for tobacco and gasoline.[16]

RECREATION AND EDUCATION

Colony leaders were particularly conscious of the need for community recreation and amusement. Shows staged by A. M. Atmore and his wife, former vaudeville actors, provided the first entertainment. A barbershop quartet, various string groups, and masquerades received much notice in the *Colonist*. During the autumn of 1917, Bray scheduled a party at his home in Fallon every two weeks, promised the young people a dancing pavilion, and bought a cider press to add "zest and pep to the evening circle of happy colonists."[17] Occasional socials were held in conjunction with the Churchill County Socialist party, and when the Farmers' Union at Fallon opened for business, the colonists contributed to the ceremonies and distinguished themselves by each wearing a large green badge. In early 1918, a literary society was organized, a motion picture machine put into operation, a garden club formed, and a Red Cross unit set up for the knitting of socks.

At times the old frontier spirit of work, fun, and cooperation caught the popular imagination. Members of the Lower Ranch on one occasion butchered twelve hogs in one day and then stayed up most of the night to process the meat. A few weeks later at a turkey-picking contest forty-five birds were plucked and prepared for market in a single evening. Later in the spring, certain persons were designated to keep watch on cold nights, and in case of frost the entire work force was called out to cover cantelope vines and other garden plants. All but the most necessary chores were discontinued during the Nevada State Fair held at Fallon every September. In both 1917 and 1918, prizes won in the livestock, poultry, and vegetable judging provided the colony with a larger number of ribbons than any other single competitor. The Lahonton Valley offered excellent fishing and hunting, and after the cutting of each crop of alfalfa, a group traveled to the colony lots at Lake Tahoe for a vacation.

Colony marriages called for a celebration, and when F. B. Harrison, the seventy-three-year-old Oklahoma doctor, married Julia Adams, the sixty-four-year-old Texas widow, Nevada City feted the couple at a party. Mrs. Harrison was so pleased by the reception that she purchased a one-thousand-dollar bond.[18] In another show of community spirit, and in direct attack upon the ten saloons of Fallon, the society circulated a petition which was signed by "every man and woman in the colony" demanding prohibition for Churchill County.[19]

Although at first anxious to organize their own school, the directors found that the nearby elementary schools met the needs for most colony children. At the Humboldt unit, the manager's wife became responsible for training the few children on the ranch. An adult was detailed to operate a carriage service from Nevada City to the Harmon elementary school, and the colony furnished a horse and buggy for any children who wished to commute to high school in Fallon. Much talk was devoted to the establishment of a kindergarten and the creation of a Montessori educational program. Several of the colonists were zealous proponents of the Montessori "method" and viewed it along with co-operation as a panacea for all of America's ills. Since Dr. Montessori stressed that an improper environment created most handicaps to learning, the colonists were certain that their ideal society would allow local children to be among the first in history to develop to their full capacity.

Always interested in education, the colony leaders were delighted when in August, 1917, they learned that H. M. Draper of Des Moines, Washington, wished to establish a training school for the community. "Daddy" Draper published the journal *Good Will*, conducted a children's orchestra, the "Jolly Entertainers," and personally financed and operated an orphanage at Des Moines. After reading the *Co-operative Colonist*, Draper became attracted by the Nevada experiment and used *Good Will* to further publicize it in articles entitled "A Real Republic" and "A True Democracy." On August 20, 1917, he traveled to Fallon and arranged with Charles H. Hancock to purchase some sixty acres of land lying along the Lincoln Highway about one quarter of a mile west of the colony hotel. When Draper returned to Washington, Bray took over the negotiations with Hancock and at the same time worked out an agreement which was approved by both Draper and the colony. Draper would train colony children, conduct a band, offer weekly entertainments, and temporarily provide the cooperators with an assembly hall in return for which the society would cultivate his land in partnership and allow him use of the commissary and other company property.[20]

Draper arrived at Nevada City with three orphan children in late October, and on November 5 made the first payment of one thousand dollars on the Hancock property. His wife and some twenty other orphans traveled to Park City, Montana, to wait until a building was completed. Draper opened the "Kid Kolony" in a 50- by 75-foot circus tent and with the help of the children converted the Hancock barn into a two-story schoolhouse–assembly hall. Several of the colony children attended the Draper school, and many others participated in his music programs. Communitywide band and orchestral performances served to bring the colonists into social contact with noncolony neighbors; and the kindly little man who loved children and music inadvertently attracted many families to Nevada City and helped to make their lives more pleasant and meaningful after they arrived. He provided Sunday evening music for the community, entertained at dances, and played a portable organ for funerals. Other orphans arrived during the winter, but colony bickering discouraged Daddy Draper, and on April 4 he closed his account with the commissary. A few weeks later he removed the "Home Sweet Home" plaque from over his door, loaded some ten youths into an old Ford truck, and headed for Montana to join his wife and the other children.

DETERIORATION

One of the factors which prompted Draper to leave the community was the many cases of typhoid, pneumonia, and other less serious illnesses which reached almost epidemic proportions during the winter of 1917–1918. Poor housing, exposure, inferior medical attention, and perhaps a contaminated well contributed to the health problems. Dr. A. C. Adams had been a candidate for congress in Oklahoma in 1916, and while at Nevada City, he demonstrated more interest in Socialist politics than in medicine. His mail-order drug purchases, paid for by the colony, consisted of quinine, oil of citronella, sulphur, mineral oil, and a patent gall cure. They seem to have contributed little to the well-being of his patients.[21] Dr. F. B. Harrison, an unlicensed experimenter also from Oklahoma, did not believe in drugs; he attached wires to the patient's head and "rapidly cranked a little red box" thereby producing a limited electrical impulse. Both Adams and Harrison were kindly gentlemen, however, and their pleasant bedside manner and quiet counsel for cooperation in all community affairs made them two of the more popular and trusted men of the colony.

The widespread sickness, the exodus of Daddy Draper, and the legal entanglements gave momentum to the ever-mounting tide of criticism and dissension. The first major attack on the colony and its leaders had been J. H. Barkley's "Nevada Colony Corporation A Fake," published in December, 1916. After Barkley was voted out of the colony, he issued the famous circular and mailed copies of the denunciation to dozens of installment members scattered throughout the United States. The brochure emphasized that there was no mattress factory, no flour mill, no ink factory, no tannery, the lands were mortgaged, the Union Security Company received a large share of the membership payments, and C. V. Eggleston was a czar. Eggleston immediately retaliated with a four-page circular letter and an article in the *Co-operative Colonist* in which Barkley was represented as "crooked, dishonest and untruthful." Eggleston claimed that an Oregon Socialist could furnish the names of "at least twenty comrades" who had been defrauded by Barkley.[22] Obviously, the colony suffered as a result of the controversy, and as more and more persons defected or were expelled, the circular tended to reappear and to be circulated by new critics of the society. Eggleston and Bray were repeatedly required to reply to letters like the one from Flora Yeaman of Caliente, Nevada: "Enclosed you will find a pamphlet entitled 'Nevada Colony Corporation A Fake.' Now I want to know about it and no fooling either. I have been honest with you and I expect the same from you. Answer me by return mail and give me proof that it is as you represented it to me."[23]

When in early 1918 Bray began to receive copies of the brochure almost daily, he brought legal action against Barkley. In February the case came before Judge C. T. Jones, and after an impressive number of former colonists testified to the accuracy of the publication, the suit was dismissed. The document was not to be further circulated through the mails, however. Bray, therefore, determined to lure colony opponents at Fallon into disobeying the order.

In January, Emaline Williams received a copy of the circular and an anonymous letter in which she was warned to make no further payments to the colony as it was directed by "a bunch of the worst thieves in the world. R. E. Bray is a brute and a dirty scoundrel and a big liar." The names of six former colonists who lived in Fallon were given as persons who would verify the accusations. Mrs. Williams forwarded a copy of the letter to Bray and at his suggestion agreed to provide the bait for Bray's trap. Therefore, she wrote the six Fallon residents for verification of the colony's dishonesty. A long-time Fallon resident and one of the first persons to leave the society supplied Mrs. Williams with her only reply, but Bray decided that it could not be used as grounds for a suit. Apparently, Sophia Baumann had sent the letter to Mrs. Williams. As Eggleston's former secretary she was in possession of much information which enabled her to wage a quiet, but effective, campaign against the colony.[24]

During the winter and spring of 1918, knowledge of the colony's problems became widespread. As a Mr. Schubert was traveling to Fallon from Klamath Falls, Oregon, in February, a fellow passenger cautioned him of the "socialist crooks" he would encounter at Nevada City. Handed a Barkley circular at Fallon and given further warning, Schubert boarded the return train for Klamath Falls without even seeing the community.[25] Other visitors traveled to Nevada City only to be sadly disappointed. After paying installments for over three months, W. A. Walker of Centerville, Iowa, decided to study the community at firsthand. Discouraged by reports in Fallon, he became even more depressed as Bray escorted him around the colony. Before Walker left Fallon on the return to Iowa he wrote a letter to Bray outlining the settlement's many defects, pointing to the injustice of misleading advertising, and asking that his investment be refunded. The letter was not answered.[26] After receiving one hundred shares of stock as a prize for selling twenty subscriptions to the *Co-operative Colonist*, William L. Achberger visited the colony during the spring of 1918. He promptly returned to his home in Elkhart, Indiana, canceled his installment membership, and severed all other connections with the organization.[27]

Women, more often than men, opposed the cooperative ideal and expressed shock at the primitive features of colony life. The early plan to attract and emancipate women through the establishment of a community kitchen, bakery, and laundry tended to be forgotten. When J. J. Weigmann and his wife arrived at Fallon, Bray showed them many courtesies and escorted them on an extended tour of the community. Dirty milk cans, an unkept commissary, and the dust and general disarray made Mrs. Weigmann ill, and when Bray insisted that her husband join the society, "she grew hysterical and fainted twice." She later fainted a third time when, at the rail junction a few miles from Fallon, her husband suggested they return to reconsider Bray's tempting offer. Since the Weigmanns had sold their jewelry store and other property at Price, Utah, they no longer had a home to which they could return. They eventually purchased a ticket for Los Angeles, determined to seek a new life in a new environment.[28]

Many installment members became disillusioned without making the trip to Nevada City, and when informed that their money would not be refunded, their response was sometimes poignant. A. Gellar of Chicago declared: "Your corporation is trying to build a cooperative colony in the name of socialism by false means and extracting ten dollar bits from innocent people. I can assure you that my ten dollars and so many others will soften the foundation of your so called socialist colony. . . ."[29]

But despite the acrid comments of a score of installment members, the majority of actual colonists moved from Nevada City with neither accusation nor protest. Indeed, many who left later returned, and single men drifted in and out of the colony with surprising informality. Family men like William Pierce found his old life as a St. Louis carpenter unbearable; after a few months he returned to cooperative living. The John G. Adamses of Sarepta, Mississippi, made a second attempt to adjust to the cooperative society. The J. J. Wood family of Fallon anxiously rejoined the colony after residing in San Francisco for ten months. Others like P. R. Trescott of Sparks gave the organization their entire savings and then after a few weeks moved on without complaint. Trescott and his son were accepted into the colony with the payment of $350 but were required to live in their own tent; and because they became ill, they accrued no cash credits at the commissary. With neither shelter nor clothes for the winter, they returned to Sparks in October, 1917. In a letter to the colony, Trescott expressed regret at having to leave and asked that the old canvas tent be forwarded to him as it could be used as a bed. Ever the humble and loyal socialist, Trescott later requested that the $350 be refunded or transferred so that it could be used by Kate Richards O'Hare of the *National Rip-Saw* in her effort to stay out of prison and oppose the war.[30]

Although weakened by many crises, it was the colony's confused and controversial position on the war which led in May, 1918, to the most tragic events ever faced by Nevada City. The antimilitary articles of Fred Warren and the ill-considered hints in the *Colonist* that men from the community would somehow not be drafted wrought havoc in the very society that was to have been spared. When war was first declared in April, 1917, the colony seemed little affected. Indeed, its philosophical doctrines seemed strengthened. Leaders like Warren had prophesied for more than a year that world turmoil would spread to America and that personal involvement could be avoided only by flight to the Nevada community. For more than nine months after the declaration of war, no one from the colony entered military service; as late as December, 1917, Bray informed prospective members that the society had not been touched by the international conflict. In early 1918, however, some seven colonists became likely draftees, and several men in important company positions left for the army.

J. H. Walters with his wife and three adult children arrived at Nevada City on May 16, 1917. As Socialist farmers from Idabel, Oklahoma, they accepted their party's stand against American participation in the war and were pleased to find many of the Nevada comrades of the same persuasion. Unfortunately, their son Paul was number ten in the draft lottery of Churchill County and was ordered to report to the court house in August, 1917. He ignored the call, and while his sisters and parents cooked, laundered, and ran the Lower Ranch Hotel, young Walters worked with Fred Venth, John Vledder, and other antiwar colonists. In March, 1918, German-born Fred Venth was assigned to the Humboldt ranch some thirty-two miles north of Fallon, and Paul Walters accompanied him to the isolated area bordering the Humboldt and Carson sinks. In early April, Venth moved to Nevada City, but young Walters remained at the Humboldt ranch.

After long delays, Sheriff Mark Wildes of Churchill County received orders to arrest Walters for draft evasion.

On several occasions Venth had boasted that he knew where the youth was hiding; therefore, he was pressed into accompanying Wildes to the Humboldt ranch area. On May 19 the sheriff, Venth, and a local prospector named Temple found Walters near the Humboldt ranch house. But the details of the meeting were never clarified. Wildes was shot in the back, left bleeding in a gulch for several hours, and eventually taken to Lovelock where he died.[31] Temple disappeared, and Venth's confused accounts indicated that young Walters was guilty of the shooting. Public feeling flared to a fever pitch. Churchill County commissioners offered a five-hundred-dollar reward for Walters' capture, local residents guaranteed five hundred dollars more, and Governor Emmet Boyle posted a state reward of one thousand dollars. Newspapers reported the shooting with banner headlines and mistakenly announced that the reward had been raised to the legal limit of five thousand dollars.[32] Governor Boyle ordered a military funeral for the sheriff and personally led the cortege.

An original posse of seventy-five persons was formed, but scores of additional "bounty hunters" joined in the search. On May 24 a party of four Indians shot and killed Walters in a salt marsh near the Humboldt ranch. The *Churchill County Standard* announced that "in the annals of the criminal history of the west, no more successful man hunt is recorded than the trailing to his death of Paul Walters, the cowardly murderer of Sheriff Mark Wildes."[33] A note was found on Walters' body asking officials to notify his parents at Nevada City. But the Walters family and other colonists were afraid to claim the body, and authorities buried the youth at the nearby railroad siding of Fanning. Talk of mob violence by a vigilante committee unnerved many in the society, and newspaper references to "loyal Hun sympathizers" provoked for the first time community hostility toward the colony. Crushed by grief and humiliation, J. H. Walters quit his post at the commissary, and without leaving a forwarding address, the family slipped away from utopia by night.[34]

During the week following the Walters shooting, another incident added to the mounting animosity toward the colony. After his withdrawal from the society, Marle Woodson became a private broker dealing in company stock, which he advertised rather extensively. As colonists left Nevada City, he purchased their stock for a few cents on the dollar and often resold it at par to unsuspecting cooperators. In late May, 1918, a sixty-two-year-old widow arrived at the colony hotel with her invalid son. Woodson, along with two other ex-colonists, had traded the woman thirty-five hundred shares of stock for her farm in eastern Texas. Bray refused to grant the unfortunate widow a work permit and transported her to Fallon where in desperation she contacted the local authorities. The three stock salesmen were called before a judge and directed to return the deed to the Texas property and to personally finance the woman's travel back to Texas.[35]

Before the unhappy developments of 1918, public opinion had not condemned the society. Nearby neighbors regularly transported individual colonists to and from Fallon, loaned them tools, employed them during busy seasons, joined them on hunting and fishing excursions, and gave them baskets of food at Christmastime. But both internal and external relations continued to deteriorate during the summer of 1918. Tempers flared in the community, and bloodshed was narrowly averted on a number of occasions.

In a fit of despondency, one colony woman committed suicide. After stock sales were discontinued on July 1, Bray typified the defeatist attitude by reasoning that if there were "no more members" there would be "no more knockers."

For the colonists, Nevada City was the cumulative weight of little details, brief encounters, formless conversations, and day-to-day behavior. The sense of comradeship with fellow workers, the excitement of gossip, the cliques, and the trivial incidents gave the community its disposition, color, and even meaning. William Pierce's shooting of H. C. Taylor's dogs, Dr. Harrison's determination to cut the old shade trees, and angry and desperate women clawing at the despised Eggleston until he sought refuge under an automobile are the things that have been remembered. As a personal experience the movement was far from ephemeral.

The colonists were not Marxists who could forego the "now" for a well-engineered utopia in the future; they were not monastically oriented stoics who were willing to save their deeper experiences for a postulated hereafter; they were not fervent optimists who could forsake the present for the promise of America; nor were they visionaries who called for "pie in the sky" rather than bread on the table. And yet the colony was a mirage which offered a heroic-sized image to which many could attach their hopes and ambitions. It was the vehicle which could deliver them from oppression and nonfulfillment.

Beliefs as diverse as trial marriage and vegetarianism, mental telepathy and teetotalism were argued. Everyone opposed mammon, which was variously interpreted as the privileged class, the capitalistic press, and the stock exchange. And for many, socialism assumed a quasi-religious character which could provide the colony with human dignity, true democracy, and social justice. Therefore, it was not only a community and an organization that failed at Nevada City but an idea and a principle. Colonists did not understand that noble ideas could be translated into effective action only through a slow and contradictory process and that principles had to be combined with a deft mastery and appreciation of the cumbersome process by which a program approaches reality.

For a few persons the colony remained a high point in their individual experience. Although unable to meet the challenges of collective society, they gloried in having made the attempt to restore purpose and direction to their otherwise meaningless lives. Fortunately, the majority of the colonists lived to understand that the enemy against which they mustered their attack was elusive and could assume many poses. They learned that the failures at Nevada City grew from the failures of their era and from the failures of human nature.

In an indefinable way the Nevada colonists were not unique; they typified the conscience and the goals of thousands of restless Americans. The colony, in a sense, was in the mainstream of American thought and experience. Its members advocated the emancipation of women, who were soon emancipated; they lamented the plight of the wage slave, who subsequently found refuge in organization; they decried the exploitation of the farmer, who found powerful support in Congress; they criticized predatory trusts and monopolies, which were increasingly brought under public supervision; they desired the subordination of religion to science, which for many rapidly assumed the place of God; and they advocated prohibition, which America soon translated into the noble experiment. In short, most of the utopian *issues* that they advanced were realized in the next generation. But their utopian *ideals* of peace, economic democracy, and social freedom eluded them in much the same way as they have eluded all mankind.

NOTES

1 *Co-operative Colonist* (Fallon), July, 1917, p. 2.

2 *Co-operative Colonist*, August, 1916, p. 10.

3 Jud Harris to C. V. Eggleston, March 13, 1917, in Miscellaneous No. 2 of the McCarran Papers in the Nevada Historical Society, Reno.

4 Bill of Sale, Fred J. Martin to Nevada Colony Corporation, June 27, 1917, in Miscellaneous No. 6 of the McCarran Papers.

5 J. B. Jenkins to W. I. DeLong, March 5, 1917, in Miscellaneous No. 2 of the McCarran Papers.

6 Breeding Advertisement and Cancelled Checks and Stallion Service in the McCarran Papers.

7 Upton Sinclair to R. E. Bray, February 6 and 19, 1918, in Miscellaneous No. 5 of the McCarran Papers.

8 *Co-operative Colonist*, February, 1918, p. 8.

9 *Churchill County Standard* (Fallon), March 6, 1918, p. 1, c. 6.

10 B. F. Chilton to R. E. Bray, May 19 and June 4, 1918, in Miscellaneous No. 7 of the McCarran Papers.

11 Scattered records in Miscellaneous No. 7 of the McCarran Papers.

12 Day Book No. 3 in the McCarran Papers.

13 File of check stubs in Miscellaneous No. 4 of the McCarran Papers.

14 Ledger A in the McCarran Papers.

15 Day Book No. 3 in the McCarran Papers.

16 *Co-operative Colonist*, November, 1917, p. 3.

17 *Co-operative Colonist*, November, 1917, p. 3.

18 *Co-operative Colonist*, December, 1917, p. 6.

19 *Co-operative Colonist*, June-July, 1918, p. 4.

[20] See the extensive correspondence between H. M. Draper and R. E. Bray, September and October, 1917, in Miscellaneous No. 8 and Miscellaneous No. 9 of the McCarran Papers.

[21] File Box in the McCarran Papers.

[22] Form letter signed "C. V. Eggleston, President, Nevada Colony Corporation" in Miscellaneous No. 6 of the McCarran Papers.

[23] Flora Yeaman to Nevada Colony Corporation, January 25, 1918, in Miscellaneous No. 1 of the McCarran Papers.

[24] See letters of Emaline Williams to R. E. Bray, February 28 through April 23, 1918, in Miscellaneous No. 9 of the McCarran Papers.

[25] J. W. Tyrell to R. E. Bray, March 6, 1918, in Miscellaneous No. 3 of the McCarran Papers.

[26] W. A. Walker to R. E. Bray, May 18, 1918, in Miscellaneous No. 9 of the McCarran Papers.

[27] William L. Achberger to R. E. Bray, April 8, 1918, in Miscellaneous No. 1 of the McCarran Papers.

[28] See letters of J. J. Wigmann to R. E. Bray, April and May, 1918, in Miscellaneous No. 9 of the McCarran Papers.

[29] A. Geller to E. N. Richardson, September 5, 1917, in Miscellaneous No. 7 of the McCarran Papers.

[30] P. R. Trescott to Nevada Colony Corporation, October 21, 1917, and February 25, 1918, in Miscellaneous No. 3 and Miscellaneous No. 9 of the McCarran Papers.

[31] *Churchill County Standard*, May 22, 1918, p. 1, c. 7.

[32] Reno *Evening Gazette*, May 23, 1918, p. 1, c. 7.

[33] *Churchill County Standard*, May 29, 1918, p. 1, cc. 1–3.

[34] R. E. Bray to J. J. Wood, June 14, 1918, in Miscellaneous No. 9 of the McCarran Papers.

[35] R. E. Bray to J. J. Wood, June 1, 1918, in Miscellaneous No. 9 of the McCarran Papers.

Chapter VI

The Search for
a Philosophy

A FEELING OF CONFIDENCE in ultimate political victory dominated the socialist movement after the formation of the Social Democratic party in 1901. The Debs-Harriman ticket of 1900 attracted fewer than one hundred thousand supporters, while in the election of 1912, the party received almost one million votes. In the era of political successes, utopian colonies were generally ignored, and men who later lauded the Nevada idea actively opposed all group experiments.

FROM NATIONAL POLITICS TO COOPERATIVE COLONIES

In his book *The Struggle for Existence*, published in 1904, Walter Thomas Mills explained that cooperative colonies could never deliver society from the hands of the capitalists. The movement had passed beyond the Bellamys and the Gronlunds. Utopian and cooperative ideals had at one point proved helpful, but they were clearly inadequate for the twentieth century. "If the co-operative commonwealth is to be inaugurated, it will not be done by capturing a township and using that to capture a continent; it will be done by capturing the political authority of the whole body of society."[1]

The decline of the Socialist party after 1912 was so rapid and the confusion and disarray so widespread that in the absence of a policy many party members reverted to the late nineteenth-century idea of cooperative societies. In 1916, Mills became a contributor to the *Co-operative Colonist* and defined Fallon as "the new socialist center of America."[2] Mills, like E. N. Richardson, Lincoln Phifer, Fred Warren, and others, accepted the Nevada colony as an unlikely, yet the only, means for preserving certain of the socialist gains. Furthermore, the Nevada experiment, through the adoption of the ideas of the Brotherhood of the Co-operative Commonwealth, held out the hope for political success at least on a statewide basis. Decay within the party was less evident in Nevada than in the East and Midwest. Indeed, the personal stature of A. Grant Miller, the legacy of radicalism at Tonopah, and the peculiar political composition of the Lahonton Valley maintained the illusion of a dynamic Nevada party until after war was declared.

In a broad sense, the Nevada colony was an outgrowth of the discouragement surrounding socialism's political failures. Fred Warren clearly set forth the feeling of frustration which led many to support the venture.

> A few days after I returned from Europe in 1914, the great war broke out. In a week the splendid Socialist Party organizations, built up after years of effort, were wiped out and the fact that socialists, syndicalists, anarchists, re-

formers and radicals alike had been forced to join the armies and were fighting . . . discouraged me so much that I resigned the editorship of *The Appeal to Reason* and concluded that there was little hope of doing anything in the United States, as I believed that the socialists and other radicals of this country would be compelled to do just as they are doing in Europe.

While I lost all hope of the Socialist Party being able to do anything of real value for the working class, I did not lose my belief in the ultimate triumph of the principles of socialism, even though they had to be worked out by capitalist governments, just as is being done in Germany and other European countries today. It was while I was in this frame of mind, that Comrade C. V. Eggleston of Fallon, Nevada, came to Girard and asked me to visit the Nevada Colony Corporation project in the wonderfully fertile Lahonton Valley.[3]

The war convinced many socialists that the Nevada colony was the proper instrument for the current emergency. Even the political activist Charles Edward Russell turned to cooperatives. Russell had once been a candidate for mayor of New York City as well as a candidate for governor and United States senator. For a few hours during the 1916 convention he was the nominee of the Socialist party for President. Yet in January, 1917, he became contributing editor for the *Co-operative Colonist* and sharply criticized the seventy-three American peace societies who proposed "to abolish war by making faces at it." Socialist colonies were to be preferred to political failures.

World courts and arbitration schemes are mere dreams. We have had all of them before. . . . Cooperation—that's the world's peacemaker; that's the thing that will abolish war. Kick out old quarrel-breeding and plague-breeding competition and bring in cooperation and you will not need a peace society anywhere. Peace will come automatically and stay forever.

So I say that you people at Fallon are doing more for peace than all the peace societies between here and the New Jerusalem. Every cooperative society is helping to bring on peace. One cooperative society, however small, does more to abolish war than a thousand Andrew Carnegies could ever do.[4]

UNCERTAIN DIRECTION

Thousands of Americans were eager to embrace the cooperative ideal. They longed for association and felt a need for material and sentimental comradeship. Whether lost in a transient and anonymous urban life, isolated on a barren western farm, or spiritually homeless in a disinterested world, they had become estranged from the body politic. They were in revolt against loss of status and the disappearance of frontier relationships. To such individuals, ownership in common, use of a commissary, and participation in the commonweal were as American as Jamestown and Plymouth Rock. Housewarmings and turkey pluckings transformed work into play. Every job in the colony stimulated the worker to his best effort because it was done cooperatively.

Those who had failed in the search for economic security particularly longed for old parochial faiths. Their expectations had been repeatedly aroused by the secular credos of free land, cheap money, and producer organizations, and they had followed charismatic leaders who promised to provide direction, restore dignity, and bring prosperity. But after a flurry of activity, all had slipped from public attention. The ever-present possibility of unemployment, the inability to provide opportunity for children, and the dread of sickness and old age were worries that could be erased by the colony.

Of course, the socialists who contributed most to the program were those who sought enduring human values. They felt the necessity to elevate mankind, and they hoped to have the lives of cooperators shaped by purpose instead of by coincidence. A cooperative was an institution designed both to share and to care.

But many confusing anomalies were quickly evident in colony doctrine. For example, Eggleston argued that while populism, muckracking, and other progressive programs had slipped from public attention, capitalism had survived seemingly unimpaired; therefore, the capitalistic system must be adapted to community purposes. Just as socialism was to be achieved through a greater utilization of the cooperative process, so was cooperation to be achieved through a proper utilization of the capitalistic method.

Eggleston and Bray also emphasized the American craving for possessions. The nineteenth century had stimulated a desire for property which was carefully exploited by the colony leaders. Publicists spoke often of the fertile fields, the prize-winning livestock, and the modern brick homes. They repeatedly explained that the payment of a few dollars gave the new colonist an equal share in the largest corporation in the state of Nevada. It was a strange anachronism. Membership in a cooperative community was advanced as the quickest way to acquire property.

Equally confusing and inconsistent was the attention given to individualism. The excitement of diversity and the stimulation gained from performing multiple jobs tended to be de-emphasized, and many persons were attracted to the community because they were offered an opportunity to specialize. A score of letters stressed the unusual skills and abilities of the writer and asked permission to develop a particular profession or trade at the colony. Publicists explained that local efficiency was an outgrowth of each person doing what he enjoyed. Only individual specialization could produce genuine cooperation. As workers came to rely on the skills and performance of fellow comrades, true interdependence would be achieved. The theorists failed to understand that they had allowed cooperation to become the by-product of individualism and specialization.

The colony never proposed isolation from the community; nor did it wish to split its allegiance like the religious groups which lived in the world but concerned themselves with spiritual as well as material issues. Nevada City viewed society as an organized system from which many classes had not received just returns. The new order was designed to gain a redistribution of privileges and rewards for its members. It would analyze weaknesses, attack obstacles, and search out possibilities for dealing with the problems of society.

The Nevada program was not based on radical new concepts nor was it dedicated to absolutes. Little emphasis was given to theoretical experimentation. No one seized upon a bold revolutionary solvent or erected a massive superstructure of doctrine. The colonists were not Rousseauists fired with an overmastering emotional ideal, anxious to treat their civilization as waste and wreckage to be swept into total oblivion. They were not dedicated to clearing the ground for an entirely new social order. Their absorption of Marxism was not permanent nor was the communist dogma consistent with their temperament. Most of the colony leaders showed a surprising uncertainty and ineptness in politics, in administration, and in socialist theory.

The organizers of the community always seemed less interested in the philosophy of the movement than in appealing to the masses and influencing the behavior of party members. They sought to clarify by oversimplification and answered questions with propaganda. They devoted little effort to social reform and seemed incapable of directing, and somewhat embarrassed by, the zeal which they often helped to kindle. They promised for day after tomorrow, houses built on foundations to be laid tomorrow. They portrayed the colony as the springtime of socialist cooperation when in actuality it was the Indian summer of a nineteenth-century dream. Although they gave assurance of a new order, they lacked the dedication and single-mindedness of either religious or utopian leaders. Their policies were contradictory, and their contributions as social agitators tended to be offset by petty foibles.

Mills, Russell, Warren, and Phifer never lived at Nevada City. They argued for action and involvement, but refused to become committed personally. They convinced many that victory could be had by heading for the Nevada frontier, but they remained behind to guard the deserted fort. Eggleston was a realistic egotist and Bray a sentimental egotist. Both were rhetorical and anti-intellectual. They deliberately cultivated people on the fringes of society, touched their needs and desires, but felt neither warmth nor obligation. They never grasped the sensitivity or compulsive hope of fellow socialists, and they consciously mismanaged the lives and fortunes of those who succumbed to their messianic call.

In short, it was a setting, not a rising, sun which the colonists pursued. They mistook emotion and propaganda for will and understanding. The new guidance and authority did not emerge from the new contacts. They floated helplessly upon a sea amidst the wreckage of wornout creeds. Their leaders misunderstood the trends and were incapable of creating order from the bewildering maze. The colony made little attempt to rise above or isolate itself from contemporary society; instead, it merely tried to profit from the wave of popular discontent. Consequently, the shifts in public opinion brought on by America's entry into the war were quickly reflected in colony philosophy.

FROM ANTIMILITARISM TO ULTRANATIONALISM

The personal and communitywide adjustments demanded by World War I tended to overshadow all other philosophical issues faced by the colony. As early as 1914, the European conflict created a dilemma in the American socialist movement. In the confusion, several socialist leaders came to champion the Nevada community, and many humble cooperators saw it as an antimilitary island isolated in a sea of chaos. But paradoxically the war stimulated the economic activity that reduced the urgency for communal life. The war also led to the canceling of all stock sales by the society, and in the Paul Walters affair, it brought personal tragedy to Nevada City. But most significant, the conflict clearly demonstrated the society's immature philosophy, nationalistic ties, and pseudoradicalism. The emergency proved that the colony was in no sense immune from patriotic sentiment or public pressures. Those who had sought personal isolation and community security in the Lahonton Valley found that they still lived in America's restless, volatile, and open society.

Throughout 1916, the *Colonist* stressed socialism and anti-militarism. An entire page was given to Fred Warren's proposed legislation on military service. He urged that: all congressmen voting for a declaration of war be drafted into the army as private soldiers and dispatched to the front; any preacher or priest who "asks God's blessing upon the success of the arms of the United States, be drafted into service as a private soldier"; all stockholders in factories supplying munitions and any editor or publisher favoring war be drafted. In case of war, Warren recommended a tax of 90 percent on all incomes over three thousand dollars per year and liberal compensation to all families furnishing conscripted men.[5] The bill was widely circulated, and the *Colonist* called for all socialists to write their congressman demanding its passage.

Articles entitled "You Fools Who Agitate for War" and "Competition, the Cause of War" bitterly attacked the American preparedness program, the invasion of Mexico, and the censorship of the press. In poems like "All Men Are Free," socialist action was demanded. The author derisively explained that Americans were free to tramp the ties, free to go to jail, free to toil and strive, and free to work and die.

> Come men! Arise! Throw off your chains
> And with your fellow workers plan;
> There's naught to lose, a world to gain,
> And Freedom here for every man![6]

The *Colonist's* revolutionary tone continued through the first part of 1917. Poems called "Comradeship," "Sunshine," and "Socialist Dream" suggested a utopian future, while the capitalistic decadence of contemporary life was revealed in "The Sucker" and "Another National Hymn."

> My stomach, 'tis of thee
> So full of misery
> Of thee I sing.
> I used to fill my craw
> With beefsteak hard to chaw,
> But now a bone I gnaw,
> Or any old thing.[7]

Anti-German statements began to appear in the *Colonist* in September and October, 1917, and by early winter the colony was in full retreat from its antimilitary stand and even from socialism. In November a fourteen-stanza poem, "Soak Der Kaiser," glorified the American fighting forces. Even Charles Edward Russell reversed his antiwar position and referred to former socialist comrades as "dirty traitors" who should "be driven out of the country." By the spring of 1918, patriotic articles and poems had completely replaced the critical tone of a year earlier. In April the spread eagle and the maiden of liberty draped in the American flag appeared in the *Colonist*, while poems like "The Traitor," "Only a Volunteer," and "Comrades, My Flag," replaced the rhymes of Jack London and the romanticized notions of *Gemeinschaften*. But even London, who in *The Iron Heel* had proposed a nationwide strike if congress declared war, became a pro-war nationalist. In May, 1918, the *Colonist* published one of his less robust poems suggesting that there would be heaven on earth when "the whole world shall be free." The community children were organized into a club "to beat the Dutch," and at the colony's second anniversary celebration in May, 1918, "America" became the theme song, used both during the program and as a closing hymn.

The success of the Socialist party and the worthiness of its program were soon called into question. The foreign elements within the party had brought on a decline that was irreversible.

> When we reflect that never has a minority party in America recovered great strength after it began to lose, it is well to look back and see what has actually been accomplished by the Marxian movement in America. . . . During the period in which Marxism was strongest in the United States, enough socialized—or public—land was diverted into private hands to create a state as large as Indiana, and this almost without protest upon the part of the movement.[8]

The *Colonist* concluded that the earlier utopian socialism, the Workingman's party, the Grange, and other organizations suggesting cooperatives had proved more effective on the American scene than the extremist European doctrines.

H. H. Stallard, the midwestern organizer and conductor of Oklahoma encampments for the colony, typified the nationalistic trend. He used the columns of the *Colonist* to condemn the Socialist party for opposing the war and suggested that the position not only was illegal and un-American, but was certain to result in the humiliation and collapse of the party. Every Socialist local in the United States was urged to take another vote on the war issue and send the results to their state headquarters so that the party could again join the mainstream of American thought.

In late January, 1918, in a page-one article entitled "Changing the Leopard's Spots," Bray announced that "the socialist leopard MUST BE TAMED. Why should this most beautiful of animals go around with a growl, showing its fangs and eternally threatening everybody and everything?" The party program must become "so beautiful and pleasing to the eye that every beholder is filled with longing to possess it." The socialist leopard had grown "wild, brutal, savage, ready to tear and rend anything and everything that came within its reach. Unable to see any of the beauties of nature around him but mad with hate because he was not master of creation." By endorsement of President Woodrow Wilson's program and by giving full support to the war, the animal would become "domesticated."[9]

Bray congratulated the *Appeal to Reason* upon its change in name and its new prowar policy. The reorganization meant that:

> The *New Appeal* will lead the movement to make the Socialist Party in this country an AMERICAN party, led by AMERICANS and inspired by the genius of AMERICAN MANHOOD; the movement shall not be prostituted to silent aid of the MAILED FIST. It means that before we can have socialism we must first have DEMOCRACY, and that the declaration of the *New Appeal* is a call to arms to maintain democracy throughout the world.[10]

The socialist leopard "will no longer snarl and show its fangs but purr and caress the hand extended to it."

Truly, Fred Warren's earlier fears that all would be lost in case of war were well founded. Both the colony leadership and Nevada socialists had eventually followed the nationalistic course, and with an enthusiasm which excelled that of their European comrades. In the election of November, 1918, M. J. Scanlan, formerly the Socialist state senator in Nevada, received only 710 votes in his bid for a seat in the United States senate. A. Grant Miller had become active in ferreting out subversive elements in his new post as a member of the Nevada Council of Defense. He later joined the Republican party. Clearly there was an inherent weakness in the American socialist and communal tradition. Almost all of the eighteenth-century religious colonies had been European inspired, and even the midnineteenth-century utopian community makers like Robert Owen, Étienne Cabet, François Fourier, Frances Wright, and Charles Lane were foreigners. America had not produced a social thinker of major rank.

The radical ideas of scientific socialism were always aimed more at autocratic political regimes than at autocratic employers. They, therefore, were less effective in America where few workers viewed the state as an enemy. Consequently, when the government called for public support in a national emergency, socialist opposition to the war melted away. Mills, Russell, Stallard, and most of the other Nevada publicists approved of the "American course" taken by the colony.

Warren was wrong, however, in assuming that a doctrine of cooperation pieced together from utopianism, Grangerism, populism, and Gronlundism could provide a vigorous defense or offer dependable protection for socialist theories. Instead of converting the state to socialism, the Nevada colony was converted to capitalism; instead of remaining an island untouched by war and violence, the colony stood condemned for the murder of Sheriff Mark Wildes; instead of growing prosperous on the land, the economic plight of the colony steadily deteriorated; instead of expanding the area of cooperative enterprise, the colony leaders became less socialistic when compelled by the war to consider how socialistic they were. Conceived in socialist failures, caught in the maelstrom of war, lacking efficient management, and led by men of little dedication, the Nevada experiment had no chance for success.

And yet "no map of the world is worth looking at unless it contains an island of utopia." Nevada City hoped to produce such an island during the harrying days of World War I. The colony failed, but failure provides meaning. The experiment demonstrated the disarray within the radical movement, the extent to which capitalism had impregnated American life, and the frustration of a generation of wage earners, petty tradesmen, and dirt farmers. For the people of Nevada City, socialism was more Christian than Marxian, and radicalism more transient than fundamental; their interests were more national than international, and their aspirations more individualistic than collective.

NOTES

[1] Walter Thomas Mills, *The Struggle for Existence* (Chicago: International School of Social Economy, 1904), pp. 249–250.

[2] Follow-up letter No. 1 in Propaganda Notebook of the McCarran Papers in the Nevada Historical Society, Reno.

[3] *Co-operative Colonist* (Fallon), July, 1916, p. 16.

[4] *Co-operative Colonist*, January-February, 1917, p. 2.

[5] *Co-operative Colonist*, July, 1916, p. 10.

[6] *Co-operative Colonist*, August, 1916, p. 14.

[7] *Co-operative Colonist*, July, 1917, p. 4.

[8] *Co-operative Colonist*, June, 1917, p. 4.

[9] *Co-operative Colonist*, January, 1918, p. 1.

[10] *Ibid.*

Appendices

DECLARATION OF PURPOSES AND PLANS
OF THE
NEVADA COLONY CORPORATION

THE OBJECT of the Nevada Colony Corporation is to organize and establish co-operative colonies to engage in agriculture, stock raising, and manufacturing industries. The capital for such industries is to be acquired from the sale of the capital stock of the Nevada Colony Corporation or from the sale of interest bearing bonds to be issued by the said Corporation.

It is provided that each stockholder of the said corporation shall be entitled to one vote for each share of stock, provided that no stockholder shall have more than twenty-five hundred votes, regardless of the amount of stock he may hold in excess of twenty-five hundred shares, this restriction to voters of its capital stock being permissible under the laws of the State of Nevada.

The said Corporation expects to engage as its employes, when it is practicable so to do, its stockholders, who shall be Caucasians, holding not less than 1,000 shares of its capital stock.

Each of its said employes so holding 1,000 or more shares of its capital stock, or who shall be the wife or husband of the owner of 1,000 shares of the said capital stock, and who shall be over the age of eighteen years, shall receive for his or her services a credit upon the books of the Corporation for $4 for each day of eight hours labor.

$1 of said credit for each day's labor, or more than $1 if the said employe so desires, shall apply as payment on additional capital stock until the said stockholder shall own 2,500 shares of the said capital stock.

Each stockholder may draw monthly, in cash, fifteen per cent of said $4 for each day's labor performed by said stockholder during said month; and the surplus earnings over and above the amount paid in stock and cash, as above provided, shall be credited to and accumulate to the personal credit of the said stockholder. Said accumulated credits to be paid out of the surplus profits of the said corporation, and not otherwise, pro rata with the amount due other employes of said corporation at the end of each fiscal year.

Each stockholder who shall be an employe shall, in addition to said $4 per day, be furnished food and shelter for himself and his wife and children under eighteen years of age during the time the said stockholder, or his wife, is at work.

It shall be the plan of the Corporation to sell to its stockholders such supplies as they may need, in addition to food and shelter, at the cost price of such supplies, or as near to the cost price as it will be practicable so to do.

It shall be the plan of the Corporation to own all of the productive property, including manufacturing or commercial industries, located at its colonies, and values created thereby shall be vested only in the Corporation. The Directors of the said Corporation shall employ managers, clerks, mechanics or other laborers that may be necessary to the management and operation of its various industries.

It is the plan of the Corporation to establish at its colonies, hospitals, laundries, libraries, auditoriums, schools, assembly halls, theatres, and places for games and amusements; all of which shall be maintained at the expense of the Corporation for the accommodation of any of its stockholders and their families, without cost to them.

It shall be the plan of the Corporation to support, at the expense of the Corporation, any of its stockholders or their wives or children, during such time as they are unable to support themselves on account of age or physical disability, provided that they have no other means of support, and provided that the said stockholder was in good health and able-bodied at the time he purchased said stock and first executed his agreement of employment with the Corporation.

Approved and adopted at a meeting of the Board of Directors of the Nevada Colony Corporation on the 1st day of May, 1916.

APPENDIX B

THE NEVADA COLONY CORPORATION, organized on the 28th day of April 1916, under the laws of the State of Nevada, with its articles of incorporation filed at Reno, in the County of Washoe, State of Nevada, and its principal office at Room 1, Journal Building, Reno, Washoe County, Nevada.

ARTICLE I. Corporate Powers.—The corporate powers of this corporation shall be vested in a governing board styled as directors, and shall at all times consist of not less than three members, which number may be changed at any stockholders meeting by a two-thirds majority vote of all the stock issued. Each director shall at all times hold one or more shares of stock in his or her own name.

ARTICLE II. Election of Directors.—The Directors shall be elected by ballot, at the annual meeting of the Stockholders to serve for one year, and until their successors are elected. Their term of office shall begin immediately after election.

ARTICLE III. Vacancies.—Vacancies in the Board of Directors shall be filled by the other Directors in office; and such Director so appointed shall hold office until the first meeting of the Stockholders thereafter.

ARTICLE IV. Power of Directors.—The Directors shall have power:

First: To call special meetings of the Stockholders when they deem it necessary. And they shall call a meeting at any time, upon the written request of Stockholders holding one-third of all the capital stock. Such meeting shall be held at the time and place designated in such call.

Second: To appoint and remove, at pleasure, all officers, agents and employes of the Corporation, prescribe their duties, fix their compensation, and require from them security for faithful service.

Third: To conduct, manage and control the affairs and business of the corporation, and to make rules and regulations, not inconsistent with the laws of the State of Nevada, or the By-Laws of the corporation, for the guidance of the officers and management of the affairs of the corporation.

Fourth: To incur indebtedness; and the note or obligation given for the same, signed officially by the President and Secretary, shall be binding of the corporation.

Fifth: Any action of the majority of the Directors, although not at a regularly called meeting, and the record thereof if assented to in writing by all the other members of the Board, shall always be as valid and effective in all respects as if passed by the Board in regular meeting.

ARTICLE V. Duties of Directors.—It shall be the duties of the Directors:

First: To cause to be kept a complete record of all their minutes and acts, and of the proceedings of the Stockholders, and present a full statement at the regular annual meeting of the Stockholders, showing in detail the assets and liabilities of the corporation, and generally the condition of its affairs. A similar statement shall be presented at any other meeting of the Stockholders, when thereto required by persons holding at least one-half of the capital stock of the corporation.

Second: To supervise all officers, agents and employes, and see that their duties are properly performed. To cause to be issued to the Stockholders, in proportion to their several interests, certificates of stock, not to exceed in the aggregate, five million dollars.

ARTICLE VI. Officers.—The officers shall be a President, Secretary, Treasurer, Vice President and Assistant Secretary, which officers shall be elected by and hold office at the pleasure of the Board of Directors. The compensation and tenure of office of all the officers of the corporation shall be fixed and determined by the Board of Directors.

ARTICLE VII. President.—The Board of Directors shall, at

their first regular meeting, elect one of their number to act as President; whose duties shall be:

First: He shall preside over all meetings of the Stockholders, and Directors, and shall have the casting vote.

Second: He shall sign, as President, all certificates of stock, and other instruments of writing which have been first approved by the Board of Directors, and shall draw checks upon the Depository.

Third: He shall call the Directors together, whenever he deems it necessary, and shall discharge such other duties as may be required of him by the Directors or By-Laws of the Corporation.

The President, or two of the Directors, may call special meetings by mailing or leaving a written or printed notice at the last known place of business, or of residence of each Director. Such service of notice shall be entered on the minutes of the corporation, and the said minutes, upon being read and approved at a subsequent meeting of the Board, shall be conclusive upon the question of service.

ARTICLE VIII. Secretary.—The Board of Directors shall select a Secretary.

First: It shall be the duty of the Secretary to keep a record of the proceedings of the Board of Directors and of the Stockholders.

Second: He shall keep the corporate seal of the Corporation and the book of blank certificates of stock, fill out and countersign all certificates issued, and make the corresponding entries in the margin of such book on such issuance; and he shall affix said corporate seal to all papers requiring a seal.

Third: He shall keep a proper Transfer Book, and a stock ledger in debit and credit form, showing the number of shares issued to and transferred by any Stockholder, and the dates of such issuance and transfer; countersign all checks drawn upon the Depositary, and discharge such other duties as pertain to his office and are prescribed by the Board of Directors.

Fourth: The Secretary shall serve all notices required either by law or the By-Laws of the Corporation; and in case of his absence, inability, refusal or neglect so to do, then such notices may be served by any person thereunto directed by the President of the corporation.

Article IX. The Treasurer.—The Treasurer shall receive and keep all the funds of the corporation and pay them out only on the check or warrant of the President, countersigned by the Secretary, and shall give such bond for the faithful discharge of his duty as may be required by the Board of Directors.

Article X. Vice President.—In the absence of the President, the Vice President shall be vested with all the powers, duties and functions of the President; and shall discharge such other duties as may be required by the Board of Directors.

Article XI. Assistant Secretary.—In the absence of the Secretary, the Assistant Secretary shall be vested with all the powers, duties and functions of the Secretary; and shall discharge such other duties as may be required by the Board of Directors.

Article XII. Books and Papers.—The books and such papers as may be placed on file by vote of the Stockholders or Directors shall at all times in business hours, be subject to the inspection of the Board of Directors and of any Stockholder.

Article XIII. Transfer of Stock.—Shares of the corporation may be transferred at any time by the holders thereof, or by attorney legally constituted, or by their legal representatives, by indorsement on the Certificate of Stock.

No surrender certificate shall be cancelled by the Secretary before a new one is issued in lieu thereof; and the Secretary shall preserve the certificate so cancelled as a voucher. If, however, a certificate shall be lost or destroyed, the Board of Directors may order a new certificate issued upon such guarantees by the parties claiming the same as they may deem satisfactory.

Article XIV. Certificates of Stock.—Certificates of stock shall be of such form and device as the Board of Directors may direct; and each certificate shall be signed by the President and countersigned by the Secretary, and express on its face that it is fully paid and non-assessable, its number, date of issuance, its par value, the number of shares for which, and the person to whom it is issued, and the location of the principal office of the corporation.

The Certificate Book shall contain a margin on which shall be entered the number, date, number of shares and name of the person expressed in the corresponding certificate.

ARTICLE XV. Corporate Seal.—The corporation shall have a corporate seal consisting of a circle, having on its circumference the words, NEVADA COLONY CORPORATION, Reno [amended November 13, 1917 to Fallon], Nevada, incorporated April 28, 1916.

ARTICLE XVI. Stockholders Meetings.—The annual meeting of the Stockholders shall be held on the 2nd Tuesday in November [amended November 13, 1917 to last Saturday] of each year, in Reno [amended to Nevada City], Nevada. All meetings of Stockholders shall be called by a notice printed in one or more newspapers published in Washoe County [amended to Churchill County], Nevada, as the Directors may direct, for at least three times and at least two weeks preceding the day of meeting, or by ten days notice in writing by the President delivered personally or mailed to each Stockholder at his last known address. The Directors shall have power to change the place of the annual meeting of Stockholders by mailing notice to each Stockholder at his last known address sixty days prior to the date of such meeting.

No meeting of Stockholders shall be competent to transact business unless a majority of stock is represented except to adjourn from day to day, or until such time as may be deemed proper.

At such annual meeting of the Stockholders, Directors for the ensuing year shall be elected by ballot, to serve for one year, and until their successors are elected and qualified. If however, for want of a quorum, or other cause, a Stockholders' meeting shall not be held on the day above named, or should the Stockholders fail to complete their elections, or such other business, as may be presented for their consideration, those present may adjourn from day to day, or until such time as may be deemed proper, until the same shall be accomplished.

ARTICLE XVII. Voting.—At all corporate meetings each Stockholder, either in person or by proxy, shall be entitled to one vote for each share of capital stock held by him, provided that no stockholder shall have more than twenty-five hundred votes, regardless of the amount of stock held by him in excess of twenty-five hundred shares, and provided that no stock can be voted which has been transferred within twenty days preceding the date of the election.

Article XVIII. Amendments.—The By-Laws may be altered or amended at any meeting of the Stockholders, by a majority vote of the stock represented at such meeting, or by a majority vote of the whole number of the Board of Directors, to be ratified by the first meeting of the Stockholders thereafter. The written consent of the owners of a two-thirds majority of the stock issued shall suffice to adopt, amend or repeal any part of these By-Laws.

We hereby certify that at a regular meeting of the Stockholders of the Nevada Colony Corporation, held in Room 1, Journal Building, on the first day of May, 1916, the foregoing By-Laws, numbering Article I. to Article XVIII., inclusive, were unanimously adopted as the By-Laws of the Nevada Colony Corporation.

signed

W. I. DeLong
President

L. V. Flowers
Secretary

Appendices

APPENDIX C

ARTICLES OF INCORPORATION
OF THE
NEVADA COLONY CORPORATION
UNDER THE LAWS OF THE STATE OF NEVADA

KNOW ALL MEN BY THESE PRESENTS: That we, the undersigned, have this day [April 25, 1916] voluntarily associated ourselves together for the purposes of forming a corporation under the laws of the State of Nevada.

AND WE HEREBY CERTIFY:

FIRST: That the name of the Corporation shall be the "NEVADA COLONY CORPORATION".

SECOND: That the place where the principal business of said Corporation is to be transacted is Room 1, Journal Building, in the City of Reno, County of Washoe, State of Nevada.

THIRD: That the purposes for which this corporation is formed are to carry on in this and the other States and Territories of the United States and elsewhere, such business as is hereinafter provided, and to acquire by deed, gift, will, grant, location, possession, claim or otherwise, lands, tenements, hereditaments, leasehold estates, easements, water and water rights, dams and dam sites for impounding water for power, irrigation and domestic purposes, stocks, bonds, evidences of debt, choses in action, franchises, privileges, patent rights and licenses, and every estate, right, title, interest and appurtenance in, to or concerning real and personal property of every name and nature, legal, equitable and to have and to hold, use and enjoy, manage, control, grant, assign, transfer and convey, encumber by mortgage, pledge, deed of trust, or otherwise dispose of the same and every part thereof or interest therein; to buy and sell real and all kinds of personal property and particularly,

(a) To receive and store personal property for compensation or hire, and to carry on a general warehouse business.

(b) To receive, hold, warehouse, insure, sell, exchange, or otherwise deal with and dispose of, for compensation, goods, wares, chattels and merchandise, as the agent of others, and in

186

its own behalf to carry on a general commission business.

(c) To borrow and lend money.

(d) To subscribe and contract for, buy, and otherwise acquire, sell, exchange, deal in and with, and dispose of stocks, bonds, securities, franchises, licenses, trade marks, patent rights, and privileges, and shares of the capital stock of this or any corporation whatever, and vote the stock so acquired of any other corporation.

(e) To incur any legal obligation, and as security for the payment or performance thereof, or to carry out or further any of the objects or ends of this corporation, to issue evidence of indebtedness, to issue, sell and hypothecate its corporate bonds, and as well to mortgage, pledge, hypothecate, or convey in trust any or all of its real or personal property and to accept as security, for or in satisfaction of the debts, obligations, of others, any kind of property and to accept as security, for or in satisfaction of the debts, obligations of others, any kind of property or lien thereon, or interest therein; and in connection to do any act or thing in the name of, or for or on behalf of this Corporation, and engage in or carry on any other business not prohibited by law, and accordingly acquire, deal in and with and dispose of any and all other kinds of property, which may be or become necessary, useful, convenient, auxiliary or appurtenant to any of the main or principal purposes of this Corporation, or be deemed advisable by its Board of Directors.

(f) To buy, sell, own and conduct apartment houses, hotels, farms, clubhouses, and country clubs.

(g) To do general merchandise business.

(h) To own and conduct a general manufacturing business, including wearing apparel, machinery, furniture, implements, cement, brick, lumber and all kinds of building materials, leather goods, paper, glass, vehicles of all descriptions, plumbing material, food of all kinds, and all things and commodities of every nature and kind.

(i) To do a general publishing business, including weekly, daily and monthly papers, magazines and books and job printing of every description.

(j) To do a general plumbing business.

(k) To establish, buy, sell, acquire and own canneries, creameries, slaughter and packing houses, operate and own the same, and to manage and dispose of their outputs.

(l) To construct, buy, sell, own, acquire, operate and dispose of street railroads, lighting, heating, or power plants, and to use, sell or dispose of the light, heat or power generated.

(m) To buy, construct, acquire, own, use, sell and dispose of pumping plants and to use or dispose of or sell the output.

Fourth: The amount of the total authorized capital stock shall be Five Million ($5,000,000) Dollars, which shall be divided in Five Million (5,000,000) Shares, and the par value of each share shall be One ($1) Dollar, and the amount of subscribed capital stock with which it will commence business is Two Thousand ($2,000) Dollars.

Fifth: The names of each of the original subscribers of the capital stock and the amount subscribed by each is as follows:

W. I. DeLong	$1,000.00
L. V. Flowers	500.00
R. E. Bray	500.00

Sixth: That the period for which said Corporation is to exist is fifty years, from and after date of its incorporation.

Seventh: The members of its governing board shall be styled directors of said Corporation, and shall consist of five directors, which number may be changed by the by-laws of the Corporation.

Eighth: No paid up stock and no stock issued as fully paid up shall ever be assessable or assessed.

Ninth: That at all elections of directors, each stockholder shall be entitled to one vote for each share of capital stock held by him to the amount of Twenty-Five Hundred Shares, or less, but any stockholder holding more than Twenty-Five Hundred Shares of capital stock shall not be entitled to more than Twenty-Five Hundred votes regardless of the amount of capital stock held by him in excess of Twenty-Five Hundred Shares.

signed

W. I. DeLong
L. V. Flowers
R. E. Bray

APPENDIX D

INSTALLMENT CONTRACT

THIS AGREEMENT, Made and entered into by and between
_____ of _____ State of
_____ the first party, and the NEVADA COLONY
CORPORATION, of Washoe County, State of Nevada, the second
party,

WITNESSETH:

That the said first party hereby purchases One Thousand
Shares of the capital stock of the Nevada Colony Corporation
at the par value of One Dollar per share, and agrees to pay there-
for as follows:

_____ Dollars ($_____), the receipt of which
is hereby acknowledged, and _____ Dollars
($_____), on the _____ day of _____, 191__,
and _____ Dollars, ($_____), or more, on
the first day of each month thereafter, until the amount of One
Thousand Dollars shall have been paid.

The said second party hereby employs and agrees to pay the
said first party Four ($4) Dollars per day; furnishing food and
shelter to the said first party, his wife and children, under eighteen years of age, during the time that the said first party, or his
wife, is at work, provided; That should the first party or his
family become unable to support themselves on account of age
or physical disability and have no other means of support, in
that event he or they shall be supported during the term of such
disability at the expense of said second party; provided further
that the said first party was able bodied and in good health at
the time of the execution of this contract.

The said second party shall furnish continuous employment
—reserving the right, at its discretion, to determine the kind and
character of the services to be rendered, and shall have full
power to discharge the said first party at any time; it being

especially understood that ownership of capital stock does not entitle the said first party to employment. The said first party shall work continuously, eight hours each day, periods of sickness excepted, provided that vacations shall be granted said first party upon first party giving ten days notice.

IT IS FURTHER AGREED, That employment herein mentioned may commence between January 1st and May 1st in the year Nineteen Hundred and Eighteen, provided the first party, prior to the commencement of such employment, shall have paid the total sum of Two Hundred Fifty Dollars for capital stock herein mentioned. Provided further, that should the first party be a married man at the time of commencement of such employment, he shall pay an additional Two Hundred Fifty Dollars in money as payment on said capital stock before food, shelter or employment shall be furnished his wife, and provided further that should the first party be a father he shall pay an additional sum of One Hundred Dollars for each child before food or shelter shall be furnished said child. Otherwise said support and employment may commence when $1000 has been paid.

It is further agreed that One Dollar of said Four Dollars (or more, if so desired by said first party) shall be paid in capital stock of the said second party, at the par value of One Dollar per share, until the said first party shall be the owner of Twenty-Five Hundred Shares of said capital stock.

It is further agreed that the said first party may draw in cash, each month, fifteen per cent of said Four Dollars for each day's labor during said month, and that the surplus earning over and above the amount paid in capital stock and cash, as above provided, shall be credited to and accumulate to the personal credit of the said first party; said accumulated credit to be paid out of the surplus profits of the said corporation, and not otherwise, pro rata with the amount due other employes of said corporation at the end of each fiscal year.

This contract may be assigned by the said first party, when assigned with all the stock and credits herein mentioned to one person only, subject to the approval of the said second party.

This is the only contract now existing between the said parties relative to the subject matter of this instrument, and the said second party shall not be responsible for any representations made, nor any agreements not incorporated herein or attached hereto.

Signed in duplicate by the parties hereto this _____ day of _____ 191__.

_____
(Party of the First Part.)
NEVADA COLONY CORPORATION
(Party of the Second Part.)
By_____
Vice-President.
By_____
Secretary.

Bibliographical Essay

SCORES OF BOOKS, periodicals, newspapers, and related references help to explain the forces which led to the formation of the Fallon society. Little of the material dealing directly with the colony, however, has previously been exploited. Basic to the study are the company records herein referred to as the Mc-Carran Papers. The collection includes twenty-eight separate units of material. Much of the contemporary correspondence as well as occasional receipts, bills of sale, proxies, mortgages, and contracts are contained in ten folders classified under the general heading of miscellaneous. The remaining eighteen units include file boxes, cash record books, ledgers, journals, minute books, propaganda notebooks, agreements, and related documents. Although most records were kept by the colony secretary, occasional statements by the treasurer, as well as reports by the president and other officials, are also preserved in the collection.

A second source of information was provided through interviews with numerous participants in the experiment, with contemporary observers, and with others intimately acquainted with the local milieu. The twenty-one persons listed in the preface were especially helpful in providing factual data and in expressing local reaction to the experiment. A third valuable area for study was the colony newspapers. The twenty issues of the *Co-operative Colonist* and the single issue of the *Nevada Colony News* collected by the University of Nevada library provide the most colorful as well as the most detailed accounts of the colony activities. Official documents found in the offices of the secretary of state and governor at Sacramento and at Carson City and the extensive county records relating to the company at Los Angeles, Reno, and Fallon provide a legal history of the society.

Other sources are so scattered that a comprehensive bibliography fails to relate to the central theme. Perhaps the chapter notes can provide the most meaningful guide to specific topics of interest.

Index

Index

Bowman, H. W.: 20
Boyle, Emmet: 157
Bray, Lillian: 125
Bray, Ralph: 125
Bray, R. E.: 69, 96, 99, 108, 119, 139, 149, 150, 152, 156, 159, 167
  character of, 74–75
  directs Colony, 74ff., 120–128
  early life, 73–74
  evaluation of, 169
  leaves Colony, 129
  nationalism of, 173–174
  opportunism of, 140–142, 153–154
  in Ozark feud, 126, 128
  promotion by, 75–80
Brazil: 31
Brock, Edward: 97
Brook Farm: 10
Brotherhood of the Co-operative Commonwealth: 3, 36, 37, 38, 39, 65, 164
Bunker, Edward: 39
Bunkerville, Nevada: 39, 43

Cabet, Étienne: 10, 175
Caliente, Nevada: 152
California, state of: 12, 13, 14, 15, 17, 18, 21, 24, 25, 26, 27, 29, 30, 31, 42, 62, 63, 64, 71, 77, 78, 79, 89, 92, 93, 98, 101, 102, 112, 115, 118, 139, 141
Calvinism: 13
Campbell, John: 97
Canada: 2, 42, 65, 72, 78, 92, 102
Canadians: 51, 81, 97
Carey Act: 45, 58n
Carithers, C. V.: 126, 129
Carnahan, H. L.: 19, 118
Carnegie, Andrew: 166
Carnegie Steel Corporation: 84
Carson City, Nevada: 35n, 42, 44

Carson Sink: 112
Carson River: 44, 48, 49
Catholics: 89
Central Pacific Railroad: 44, 45
Cherokee County, Kansas: 76
Cheyney, Edward P.: 76
Chicago, Illinois: 38, 76, 154
China: 98
Christian Commonwealth Colony: 37
Christian Socialism: 12
Christian Socialists: 103
Churchill County Eagle: 61
Churchill County, Nevada: 24, 26, 28, 53, 54, 55, 57, 61, 62, 69, 110, 111, 112, 147, 148, 156, 157
Churchill County Standard: 61, 141, 157
Cohn, Morris: 42
Collier's Weekly: 97
Colorado, state of: 38, 53, 98, 138
Columbia River: 100
Coming Events: 74
Coming Nation: 65
Comstock, Frederic: 97
Congregationalism: 12
Cornell State Agricultural School: 118
Constructive Socialist: 74
Cooperative colonies: 9ff., 87
Co-operative Colonist: 66, 69, 71, 72, 73, 75, 77, 78, 83, 84, 85, 88, 90, 93, 103, 119, 126, 129, 137, 139, 140, 141, 147, 149, 152, 154, 155, 164, 165, 171, 172, 173
The Cooperative Commonwealth: 3, 36
Co-operative Consumer: 75
Cooperative Herald: 76
Co-Operative News: 75, 76
Corey Army: 15
Corporate Securities Act: 19

Index

Index

Index

Indianapolis, Indiana: 14
Industrial Workers of the World: 15
Inman, F. W.: 137
International School of Social Economy: 64
Iola, Kansas: 53
Iowa, state of: 153
Iron Heel: 172
Isle of Pines, Cuba: 31, 98
Italian-Swiss Colony: 12
Ivanuck, Paul: 98

Jackson, Adam: 80
Jacksonianism: 43
Jang, O. S.: 93
Japanese colony: 12
Jenkins, J. D.: 138
Jewish colony: 41ff.
Jones, C. T.: 152
Jones, Senator John P.: 44
Jordan, David Starr: 89
Jordan, Fred: 138

Kansas City, Missouri: 65
Kansas City Times: 69
Kansas, state of: 53, 67, 70, 74, 75, 79, 83, 100, 103, 141
Kent Company, I. H.: 131
Kentucky, state of: 138
"Kid Kolony": 150
King, C. A.: 21
Kline, C. T.: 96
Kolstrup, R. J.: 96
Kopf, Anna: 99
Kormier, John: 96, 100, 101

Labor-Socialist party: 51
Lahonton Dam: 48, 54
Lahonton Valley: 2, 48, 55, 64, 71, 89, 91, 98, 102, 126, 128, 131, 148, 164, 165, 171

Lake Tahoe: 112, 148
Lancaster County, Pennsylvania: 88
Lane, Charles: 175
Lang, Chard: 137, 138
Lassen County, California: 110, 111
Leader: 75
Leesville, Louisiana: 30
Lemmon Valley, Nevada: 41
Lincoln Highway: 113, 135, 138, 149
Linsey, Ben: 89
Lippmann, Walter: 76
Llano Colony: 3, 13, 20, 21, 23, 24, 25, 26, 30, 31, 33, 36, 61, 71, 74, 87, 98, 118
    collapse of, 28
    move to Louisiana, 29
    organization of, 15ff.
    publicity of, 18–19
Llano del Rio Company of California: 16, 17, 18, 24, 25, 26, 35n
Llano del Rio Company of Nevada: 26, 27, 31, 32
London, Jack: 172
Looking Backward: 11
Los Angeles, California: 12, 14, 15, 16, 18, 20, 21, 22, 23, 24, 25, 26, 31, 62, 87, 154
Los Angeles Times: 14
Louisiana, state of: 19, 29, 30, 31, 87
Lovelock, Nevada: 97, 157
Lower Ranch: 113, 122, 148, 156
Lutherans: 101, 102
Lyon County, Nevada: 42

Maine, state of: 37
Malays: 19
Manhattan, Nevada: 51
Markham, Edwin: 18

Index

Index

Index